Cycling Heroes
The Golden Years

In memory of my old pal, Gayf

Les Woodland

Cycling Heroes

The Golden Years

SBL Springfield Books Limited

This edition first published by Springfield Books Limited, Norman Road, Denby Dale, Huddersfield HD8 8TH, West Yorkshire, England.

First edition 1994

Photo credits

The author and publishers wish to thank the following:

Presse Sports for photographs on the cover, left and centre, pages 85, 119, I, III (lower), VI (upper), VII, VIII (lower), X (both) XI, XIV (lower), XV (both), XVI (upper left), XVI (upper right);

Photosport International cover, right.

British Library Cataloguing in Publication Data

A catalogue record for this book is available from the British Library.

Editing, design and layout: White Line Publishing Services, Leeds.

Origination: Sele & Color, Bergamo, Italy.

Printed and bound in Italy by: Tipografia Umbra, Citta' di Castello.

CONTENTS

1 A JOURNEY THROUGH TIME

De fiets is te klein voor u!

Everywhere I went, they told me the same thing: *De fiets is te klein voor u!* — or *Le vélo, c'est trop p'tit!* The bike is too small for you.

When you're 6ft 2in, even a 23-incher looks like a key ring. But there's no point in arguing with 13 million Dutchmen.

That old Carlton and I had been together for 15 years, since it was lifted from a hook in a bike shop in Peterborough. This was a nostalgia trip, to heroes who used to gaze unreachably from magazines like *Miroir Sprint*. The latest, polished works of Italian bike factories would have been as out of place as techno-pop, gaudy training tops and fizzy lager. I would revel in my past in my own way.

That was when news of foreign cycling meant occasional hope of hearing Jock Wadley telephoning with some difficulty from France on Network Three. But then who remembers Network Three? It was an enclave within the Third Programme before it became Radio 3. Wadley had to book his telephone call hours in advance, and men with donnish looks and heavy books would sigh and allow the ruffians in among Mozart and Mendelssohn. Wadley stood in call-boxes to announce that Tom Simpson had won Bordeaux–Paris, or that some foreigner with a difficult name was the new world champion.

I recall television's contribution being little more than static coverage of the Tour of Britain, including a government minister famously waving the competitors away with the words 'Have a good rally, lads.'

You don't have to be terribly old to remember such things. Forty would be plenty enough. That would take you back to Continental magazines with big pictures in clumsy colours. They relished crumpled heroes at the roadside, clutching their heads, streaming with blood. The inevitable words in the caption were *chute terrible*. They are as unforgettable as Horace Bachelor, the Infra-Draw pools system and his painfully pedantic spelling of K-e-y-n-s-h-a-m.

And so I thought I'd go back. I'd go and see some of these old guys. I would rest my bike against their garden gates and walk in with a tape recorder. In some cases I did it for *Cycling* magazine but in others it was simply for pleasure.

I couldn't see them all, of course. They were too far away, or sometimes they weren't there, or time got there first. With them, I've had to rely on records and recollections. And that just made me more glad I saw the ones that I saw. A few more years and leather saddles and woollen vests and tyres around the shoulders will have gone for ever.

2 PETER POST (1933–)

Trains in Holland are blue and yellow, with adverts on the side.

D-A-A-G!, one of them says in huge wavy capitals. It means 'day', but it can also mean 'good morning' or even 'goodbye'. In the advert for *De Telegraaf*, the paper with big underscored head-lines published in Amsterdam, it's writ-ten wavily because that's how the Dutch say it — like a two-tone car hooter, first up and then down. The Belgians, who also speak Dutch but call it Flemish, find this very funny.

The Dutch also make the last letter so guttural that it coughs, the Belgians preferring their Gs like an H.

There were several of these trains at Hoek van Holland station, some with *fiet-senrijtuigen* (bike carriages) into which

young people with heavy bikes, books and large, milk-white teeth pushed their bikes before taking their place. The Dutch don't, as a matter of course, commute long distances; to travel more than five miles is extraordinary. These were students returning to Leiden after the weekend.

I bought coffee in the station restaurant, crossed the tracks, picked up the first of the white toadstools with their instructions to cyclists written in red, and followed the old sheet six of the Michelin map. However new your map, it is always out of date. This over-crowded country is for ever building roads. More than that, many main roads are closed to bikes, and signposting for cyclists is restricted to unheard-of suburbs rather than distant towns.

Lunch was in Noordwijk, sheltering over the eggs and ham of an *uitsmijter* as the wind blew froth off the North Sea. Then the battered tulip fields of Keukenhof, denuded now of their Women's Institute broad-beamed ladies, and on across Haarlemmer Meer wastelands to Amstelveen.

I'd seen Peter Post before, at the six-days in north London. First he'd been a rider, later an organiser. Everyone said he was a bastard.

'It is a fine thing,' the *New York Times* said in 1897, 'that a man astride two wheels can, in a six-day race, distance a hound, horse or locomotive. It confirms the assumption, no longer much contested, that the human animal is superior to the other animals.

'But this undisputed thing is being said in a too solemn and painful way at Madison Square Garden. An athletic contest in which the participants "go queer" in their heads, and strain their powers until their faces become hideous with the tortures that rack them, is not sport. It is brutality.

'It appears from the reports of this singular performance that some of the bicycle riders have actually become temporarily insane during the contest, while all of them are sore, cross, and distorted. Permanent injury is likely to result from the attempt to perform any task that is beyond the limits of what a man can undergo and make up for in one night's sleep.

'Days and weeks of recuperation will be needed to put the Garden racers in condition, and it is likely that some of them will never recover from the strain.'

And they were right. Some really did go 'queer in their heads' and a few never recovered. A spectator arriving on the fourth day asked why one rider crouched over his handlebars each lap.

'Ah,' said the colleague, 'the silly fool thinks there's a low bridge there.'

That's what you get when you've been doped with cocaine and alcohol and driven beyond the point of reason for money. No wonder common decency demanded an end. It came, just as it did to dance-'til-you-drop jive marathons and last-man-upright-wins skating sessions. A world which tolerated freak shows had passed. And in 1899, two years after the *New York Times* reporter returned shocked to his office, the law stepped in. The sight of men pedalling 1,400 miles in six days, their legs festered and bloody from untreated splinters stripped from the wooden track by crashes, was past.

Within weeks, the races were reborn, the agony alleviated by sharing the work in two-man teams. But the speed increased and the opportunity for sleep barely grew. The two-man formula was named after the very venue which had seen the demise of its predecessor: the madison. It was good downmarket enter-tainment, excitement for the hot-dog classes, seedy and almost safe, like a flap-per track where neither the dogs nor the bookies use their real names.

'Jams' could last for hours. It was dangerous and highly paid. Alf Goullet was getting $1,000 a day in 1926, and where a rider covered 3,300km alone in 1891, a pair could now be riding 4,500km between them.

In 1926 Goullet — whose trademark was a silk scarlet jersey with black trim on the sleeves — wrote that a six 'is the most gruelling contest in athletics because of its sheer monotony. If we weren't mercifully built that we quickly forget our sufferings, I don't believe there is a man in the world who would ride in more than one. It takes toll of every muscle in the body, of the stomach, of the heart. In the past 15 years, I have ridden in 24 and the only way I can think of describing the riding is as one infernal grind.'

The cacophony was appalling. The actress Peggy Joyce gave $200 primes whenever she thought the action was flagging. Sometimes there could be several bands playing in the stadium at the same time, and when one struck up 'Pretty Peggy with Eyes of Blue' she surpassed herself with a single prime of $1,000 — maybe £5,000 or more nowadays. Bing Crosby paid the hospital bills of those who crashed in the attempt.

And crashes were popular. In France, the crowds were entertained by a shrewd old runner — a foot athlete — called Georges Berretrot. It was he who dreamed up the idea of asking the public for extra money, bonuses or *primes* to offer as a reward or an inducement. He could also manipulate them.

Many had paid sizeable amounts to watch Jean Brunier in action. But Brunier was a road rider, the current champion, and a disappointment on the boards. When Berretrot sensed the crowd getting restless after yet another crash, he left the microphone and popped down to see Brunier in his cabin.

'Next time you crash,' he told him, 'stick on the biggest plaster you can find, even if the injury's really quite minor. I'll get sympathy for you and we'll both profit.' Berretrot was on a percentage of the takings, which included the primes.

'Agreed!' Brunier laughed, and he fell off at least another 15 times, usually quite voluntarily. Each time, Berretrot picked up his microphone and appealed: 'Look at that poor courageous Brunier! Let's help him. A little prime will help his suffering!' And the money rolled in.

The original Madison Square Garden closed on May 5, 1925. Eight and a half years later, on November 12, 1933, Peter Post was born in Amstelveen.

He rode his first six in 1956 and won his first two years later. From there on he matched Torchy Peden's 38 successes, then Rik van Steenbergen's 40, until he finally accumulated 65.

I first saw him at Earls Court, the first of the new London sixes, my mates and I wondering whether he would accept 10 bob to have his picture taken in a Westerley Road Club hat. We never picked up the courage to ask.

He lives in a light-coloured bungalow, a luxurious one, on a corner. The address is no secret. He's in the Amsterdam phone book and it's the address you see when cycling magazines detail Continental bike teams. Cobe Ritsemahof is named after an old painter. It's the last street before Amstelveen — where Post had a ten-pin bowling alley that burned down — becomes Amsterdam.

I went to number 15 first. A lady in a smart dress sent me five doors down the road in Dutch as educated as a radio newsreader's. In egalitarian Holland, this area is clearly a little more egalitarian than the rest.

There was a red Mercedes outside No. 5 and a white team-car run-around. Post was late. I was invited to bring my bike indoors, and Post, when he arrived with his shoulders held permanently high like a great bear, marvelled that I had cycled 60 miles to see him. This from a man whose riders race two and a half times as far — and rather faster.

It was a tasteful modern room, painted in those warm but neutral creams you find in every Novotel, Eurotel and Comfotel in Europe. Perhaps it says something of his life. A large white desk had two telephones on one side, partly obscured by a potted plant. There was a pile of team jerseys and a television. The moment he came in, he checked the financial news.

'The English pound fell a couple of cents today,' he said. He could tell you the exchange rate of a dozen different countries.

Once, also on television, I saw Post completing some big race; he turned left instead of right when he entered the track on which it finished. Odd, I thought, for a man who went on to earn a fortune on the track. But I kept my thoughts to myself.

'The six-days were paid well enough,' he said. 'Not a lot, but not badly either. I enjoyed them. They were exciting, in a sporting sense. And pretty tiring, too. I mean, in the first years, you were riding all the time, hardly sleeping, in the real six-days. You'd ride eight of those real sixes in a winter. There weren't any more, anyway. But you couldn't ride more than eight because they were too exhausting. You could only ride one every two weeks. You actually needed a whole week to recover. You really had to sleep.

'The later sixes [with racing only in the evenings], you could ride 12, 14, straight after each other. It's totally changed.'

I took my life in my hands.

'There are people who say that you and Patrick Sercu ... how shall I put it? ... controlled six-day racing?'

He paused. '*Jawel.* Yes, we did. It's true.'

I'd meant 'controlled' in the sense of the races being predictable or even, well, fixed. I think he took it that I meant the races had been checked for their organisation, as if Post and Sercu were shop stewards of a riders' union.

So to hint at what I meant, I said: 'In what way?'

And he said: 'Well, you know, there always have to be riders prepared to say what's going to happen, that the races should be better. You have to keep discipline, to give an example.'

'And say that Peter Post had to win?'

'No, not to win. There's no point. If you were one of the top riders and you were strong enough, you could win anyway. But in those days there were so many riders who could win. But first they had to prove it.'

Once, when Post was in London, he and a blond American called Jackie Simes collided on the track and fell to the bottom. There, to make matters worse, Tony Gowland smacked into Post's back. The greatest injury was to Post's pride and he accused Simes of causing the accident. A huge row followed and Simes took a swing at the Dutchman.

It was an unwise move, regardless of fault. Simes left the race that night, blackballed for the rest of the season, and shortly afterwards packed his bags and returned to the States.

In those days you could put Post with Sercu and still get a good race. Now, I suggested, they would rip the field apart. He didn't agree.

'There were more good riders then, but you've got to remember that one couple will always be better than the rest.' Tony Doyle and Danny Clark, he suggested, were like Post and Sercu. Good enough, at any rate, for some organisers to hesitate before putting them together.

'But better?' I asked.

'I don't know. They're just a good couple. They might be as good, they might be better. I don't know.'

That revival 'six' in London in 1967 had angles in the bankings, like the inside of an old threepenny bit. Rumours said everyone was on limited gears to avoid drubbing the home professionals — good, honest but out-of-their-depth chaps like Dave Bonner and George Halls.

'Well, I've got to say it was a fine six-day. It appealed to me because it was in a good city. The name, London. It's international. It's one of the biggest cities in the world. Six-day of London, six-day of Paris, six-day of New York …'

He went on eulogising and getting nostalgic, denying that he said it because I'm an Englishman, and then I reminded him about the problems.

'Oh yes,' he said with a smile. 'We certainly had a few problems that year. That was Charles Ruys that year, wasn't it? There wasn't so much money and the organisation didn't quite come together. But it got a lot better with Ron Webb. Every night we were sprinting for a car. That was great and he was a good organiser.'

Nobody who met Ruys could forget his spectacular command of English swearwords; nobody who saw his race could forget the booming announcements, *'Tien pond voor de eerste ronde!'* — £10 for the next lap. It seemed a fortune; the riders must have sniggered at these naive Englishmen who emptied their pockets of loose change and managed no more than £10 a throw between them.

After 1967 they took the track to Calshot, on a spur in the sea near Southampton, still with its threepenny corners. It was that track, Post said, that brought the limited gears more than any fear of brave but inexperienced riders being ridden off the track.

'We had to limit the gears, I know. The English, *ja* ... they were a bit ... but soon we could see that it was going to be all right.'

I went every night and lived on hot-dogs. Every so often the English fell off.

'You know,' I said, 'people say you're not the easiest man to get along with. They say you're a good friend but a terrible enemy.'

He shrugged. He was tired. After a while he said: 'I'm not always the easiest on myself either. I don't think it's possible to be a nice guy in cycling these days. And if you're responsible for a team, for the money, then you've got to say something. And if you've got to say something to a rider ... if he's not going well, well, you've got to say so.

'Most riders don't want to know the truth, but I'm hard on myself as well. You mustn't look for the easy way out.'

'So,' I ask, 'you see the riders as what — friends? Employees?'

'Not as friends. *Werknemers*, employees. They're not my friends. But I try to have a good relationship with them. And you can relate to some riders more than others. They're all different.'

Post, in jacket and jeans, stretched for coffee which his wife, whom he calls Treasure, had left on a tray before disappearing with a friend. The Dutch drink coffee with evaporated milk, called simply *koffiemelk*. We sipped for a while, side by side on a big leather settee. There were large impressions of moto-cross and American football on one wall and a life-size painting of a Raleigh rider, arms aloft, on another. Beside it was an exercise bike.

'I don't ride a bike any more,' he said. 'Got no appeal now.'

There is more money in Dutch racing now than for many years. These are probably the best days for the game — or at least they were until the recession of the 1990s made the whole world look less of a safe bet. Or maybe, I thought, Post would think the Fifties and the Sixties were the glory era?

'No, no,' he said, 'I think that the last 12 years or so have been the best.'

That was just about the time he had been a team leader. He agreed.

'I have had some good riders. But before that, there was Jan Janssen and there was Joop Zoetemelk ... and then Kuiper, Raas, Knetemann, Karstens. They were pretty good riders.'

That large mural of the Raleigh rider might have been on the wall because it was the only one he had, but I suspect it has stayed because those years with Raleigh were the most successful he has ever had. Hennie Kuiper, for example, has little time for his former boss, and even he agrees that the Raleigh decade was a formidable one.

Well, yes. But not as good as it was. Once he would have scooped up any rider in Holland worth having and consigned the rest to racing around clock towers. When Raleigh was at its best, the other teams were minnows, like Jet Star Jeans, gone and gratefully forgotten.

Post was the first of a new breed of managers. Like many, he came from the saddle himself. He could talk like an insider. But he came, too, from business. It was once the way that cycling managers were like the bosses of old-time boxing stables, men with scarred legs instead of bent noses but with the same dat's-my-boy attitude to management and a money-out-the-back-pocket attitude to wages.

Raleigh picked him unproven. Until then, it was synonymous with single-gear clunkers with front baskets and gentlemen with bowler hats and rolled-up copies of the *Daily Telegraph*. It had employed Norman Sheil, Reg Harris and Hugh Porter to win world titles, but that was in the track era and tracks had become as empty as a tram depot on half-day closing. Sheil, Harris and Porter were fine talents, but just birds of brilliant plumage blown onto the Continent for brief and uncomfortable visits.

Raleigh had no intention of remaining the keeper of attractive but rarely-seen songbirds.

Post, whether he wanted them or not, was obliged to take on a handful of British professionals to go with his Dutchmen. They went — Brian Jolly, Phil Bayton, Bob Carey, Dave Lloyd and the rest — and one by one they came home amid tales of what a difficult old sod Post was.

Being British, we took it as a plot. Being British, we suspected it might even be true that our fellow Brits were being given the rickety chainsets and worn-out head bearings, and we took it as an insult that Post, who speaks reasonable English but only as a foreigner, found it more comfortable speaking Dutch in Holland to a largely Dutch team.

From Post's side, the story is different. He tells of riders who wouldn't try, had chips on their shoulders, just couldn't make the grade.

You end up listening to both sides, shrugging and then going away. In the end, Post had a team of Dutch-speakers salted with the occasional German. Bob Cary, who learned Dutch at evening classes in north London, lasted longer than most.

Raleigh would like to have sold more bikes in France, but Frenchmen in Team Raleigh were as common as green in the Dutch flag. The closest was Joop Zoetemelk, who has a French wife and lives in Paris. A Raleigh insider told me once that he had given up hope that the French were likely to get on with Post. Perhaps that says something, too, about the fate of the British.

Before Post became a manager, his inspiration was Gerrit Schulte, a track-ie, just as Post was to become. Post was there just at the right time, when the track paid best. Swanky houses and red Mercedes don't come from nowhere.

'Did it make you a rich man?' I asked.

'I don't know what you think of as rich,' he countered. 'I'm rich in health, that I can do anything, that I can work every day. But *ja*, if you've been working for the best part of 30 years, seven days a week, it stands to reason that you'll earn something.

'I think I just love cycle-racing in general. It's a beautiful sport. It's a sport for hard people. You've got to have a good mentality.'

'When I won Paris–Roubaix, it was certainly *geweldig* [marvellous]. My 65 six-days were also quite something for me. *Ja*. But it can't go on for ever. I was 38 when I stopped. I'd had my time. You can't race on for ever, can you?'

I stood up, stretching my back after its time in the sofa, and slung the tape recorder over my shoulder. There were the usual words of thanks and goodbye, and then he had an idea. He'd enjoyed the interview, he said, and he'd ring up a few old pals.

'Are you planning to see Jan Derksen?' he asked, moving to the big desk with its two phones. He pronounced the old sprinter's name with a silent final 'n', as the Dutch do when they're speaking colloquially.

He dialled and announced himself as Peter — pronounced 'Péter'. But Derksen was off to a funeral next day and couldn't see me then. Post scribbled his number on a scrap of card and gave it to me for next time. He didn't strike me like a bastard. Maybe it would have been different if I'd been a rider.

I never did ask him about that ten bob for a picture. But as I rode back in the darkness to my hotel, I recalled how *Cycling* had billed him amid much excitement for that opening London six. And I recalled, too, how the programme had had to be rejigged at the last moment because Tom Simpson, the one Briton who might have challenged him there, had died unusually a few days previously.

3 TOM SIMPSON (1937–1967)

I saw Tom Simpson twice in London, once when he lapped all the British semi-professionals on the motorcycle circuit at Crystal Palace, and once when a cocky south Londoner called Dave Bonner got his revenge at Herne Hill.

The only other time away from the Continent was at Douglas in the Isle of Man, where he sold me a red and white silk jersey. It was still unwashed by the smell of it, and bore the number seven he carried in a six-day race the previous winter.

A few days later, Tom Simpson was dead.

In the files of *Cycling Weekly* is a letter written by a lad of 14 who idolised Fausto Coppi and wanted to be like him. It asks for advice and it's signed Thomas Simpson. He had been racing for a year with Harworth Cycling Club, along with his brother Harry. His first race, over five miles, was in 17 minutes and 50 seconds.

He was criticised for arrogance or over-excitement whenever he won — fair criticism according to contemporaries — and he left for the Scala Wheelers. That was a Yorkshire club and he never shook off the tag of Yorkshireman. This had curious consequences. Simpson received his award as sports personality of the year from the prime minister, Harold Wilson, who made much of being a Yorkshireman. Moments before basing his speech on Yorkshire, Wilson asked Simpson where in the county he came from. Hurried rewriting followed when Simpson explained he was a north-easterner who lived in Nottinghamshire.

Simpson said jokingly in his own speech: 'I'm very pleased that Marion Coates [a horse rider] is sportswoman of the year, because we've got something in common, along with the right honourable prime minister: we're all in the saddle. I only hope their behinds don't ache like mine at times.'

Harry Simpson stopped cycling to play professional football for Blackpool. Tom, too, came close to giving up after flying through a halt sign in a race. The police caught him and the cycling authorities banned him from racing for six months.

Arrogance merged with dismay, and he bought a motorbike and sidecar to take up trials riding. He advertised his bike for £25. But as it turned out, the best offer was £20, which left him £5 short. He hadn't made up the £5 by the time the suspension ended, and the future world champion drifted back into cycling.

He asked George Berger, a French-speaker in the Redhill club in Surrey, to translate Louison Bobet's book *En Selle*, and set out to be a roadman. But at the Brodworth Sports, someone suggested Simpson should look not there but the track.

On June 23 he won a 4km pursuit by a second, finishing with a red throat and a furious, barking cough. And within half an hour he'd been introduced to the former champion and world championship silver medallist, Cyril Cartwright, famous for his crouching style.

Cartwright said: 'I rode around with him, showing him how to ride the bike, tactics, how to get in a winning position, how to get off the mark quickly, how to ride dirty, how to avoid being brought off, how to train, how to develop a good sprint finish.'

'He was always on the phone to me and he was hungry for knowledge.'

The guru's influence was astonishing. Simpson moved to Fallowfield in Manchester for eight days before the national pursuit championship, training on the road in the morning with some visiting Americans and Australians and then on the track in the afternoon with the same lads and Reg Harris.

Simpson said: 'It was much harder than I had been used to, and after three days I was just about dead, but I gradually picked up over the week and somehow got fit.'

The results in the title series were spectacular. First he beat Pete Brotherton, the previous year's silver medallist. Then he eliminated the world champion, Norman Sheil.

Inspired now, and turning his arrogance to full benefit, he narrowly beat John Geddes in the semi to meet Mike Gambrill in the final. But there two punctures and mental tiredness defeated him, and Gambrill won the gold.

Simpson did finally win the pursuit title, in 1957, and he got within 350 metres of the world hour record in Switzerland. But a worrying trend developed. Put simply, Simpson fell off a lot. He was a skylarker, wandering through the women's showers in Bulgaria, punching his Olympic boater into a bowler at the opening ceremony in Australia, drawing protests in Russia after being dunked in a river in Leningrad, and being arrested in Rumania without a visa. But there was a deeper, self-destructive trend which saw him not simply riding to his limit but crashing on finishing lines (he dislocated his jaw, alone at the end of a qualifying pursuit heat in the 1958 world championship), all but destroying himself in races.

He was not strong or big enough for this self-abuse.

One of his closest friends, Vin Denson, knew Simpson was more brave than athletic. He told me: 'We often used to have a laugh with Tom about his hollow chest. It was considered to be hereditary, because with his family's mining history, and the lack of oxygen down in the pits, all their lungs were underdeveloped. He had a really good pair of athletic legs, but his chest was always a worry to us. We never ever thought that he did actually get sufficient oxygen in the tiny lungs that he must have had.

'In the shower, for instance, we used to have a giggle at him because of his concave chest.'

This spindly Englishman took £100 to Brittany soon after Easter 1959, first to race, and second to escape a compulsory spell in the armed forces. He applied for a semi-professional licence in his first year, and within another year had his first professional contract.

But an Englishman abroad has pressures that domestic riders never face. The French had homes and families to support them, and the enthusiasm of local crowds, and the chauvinistic wish of the French to see another Frenchman win. More, a rule forbade professional teams to have more than a small percentage of foreign riders, which meant that throughout his career — there being no British team on the Continent — Simpson had to displace French riders from French teams to secure his own place.

This is not a formula for a relaxed frame of mind, and, while Simpson had quietened down a little, he was rarely relaxed on his bike.

Jacques Goddet, the pith-helmeted and shorts-wearing organiser of the Tour de France, said of him after his death: 'A champion, he wanted victory too badly. We often asked ourselves if this athlete, who at his work often appeared in pain, had not committed some errors in his manner of looking after himself.'

Simpson won 28 races in his first year as a pro. He was a trier. Some of his efforts might have been vainglorious, in the grand style, but what they denied him in triumphs they brought him in attention, which secured team places against those domestic favourites. He spent 40 miles alone in his first Milan–San Remo before being caught on the Poggio climb just before the finish. He led Paris–Roubaix for 56 minutes in the year it was first shown on Eurovision — and lost the race two miles from Roubaix.

He finished his first Tour de France a wreck, having crashed in Brussels on the first day, and so over-did the richly paying village races afterwards that he ended up in hospital in Paris to recuperate.

There *were* glory days, of course. Lots. He won the Tour of Flanders in 1961, the first Briton to win a classic since the 19th century. But then came a spell when he didn't win for two years. It was an odd pattern. And all of it characteristic of what Goddet had said about 'some errors in his manner of looking after himself.'

Simpson was not the first to take drugs. Nor was he alone. As Alan Gayfer, the former editor of *Cycling*, put it: 'They were all on it.' Simpson's closest supporter in Belgium, Albert Beurick, told me: 'I know he took them. But he didn't take them all the time. It wasn't drugs, drugs, drugs.'

And yet the world sprint champion Reg Harris also told me: 'Simpson was a stupid boy. Stupid. He would take drugs in training, let alone in racing, just to see how he went on them.'

In his book *Tom Simpson*, Roger St Pierre quoted Simpson as saying: 'I don't like using drugs, but if not taking them means being beaten by riders who I know are not as good as me, then I shall have to forget principles. You see, I have a wife and family to support and no victories means no money.'

But it's also worth remembering that, in that era, behaviour like this was by no means unusual, however hypocritical the offenders might have been in public, professing innocence or wringing their hands in regret.

Pierre Dumas reported the comments of Marcel Bidot, manager of the French team during the 1960 Tour: 'Three-quarters of the riders are doped. I am well placed to know since I visit their rooms each evening during the Tour. I always leave frightened after these visits.'

Dutch team manager Kees Pellenaars recounted how he had raided the cupboard of a young rider trying to impress him at a training camp.

'With a *soigneur* and another rider, we counted the pills: there were five thousand of them, excluding hormone preparations and sleeping pills. I took the five thousand bombs away, to his own relief. I let him keep the hormones and the sleeping pills. Later, he seemed to have taken too many at once and he slept for a couple of days on end. We couldn't wake him up.

'We took him to hospital and they pumped out his stomach. They tied him to his bed to prevent anything going wrong. But somehow or other he had some stimulant and fancied taking a walk. A nurse came across him in the corridor, walking along with the bed strapped to his back.'

Don't rush to make judgements, unless it's to dismiss the folly of those days. Cheating is to take unfair advantage. When everybody used drugs, there was no advantage. There was stupidity and medical ignorance and official connivance and often sheer greed, but the world has rarely been otherwise.

After 18 months without a win, Simpson came back suddenly. He strode across the Pyrénées between Pau and St-Gaudens in 1962 to wear the *maillot jaune* for a day in the Tour de France. And in 1963 he dominated Liège–Bastogne–Liège, but was caught and dropped by the bunch a mile from the end. Then he won the 356-mile Bordeaux–Paris by five minutes. In 1964 he won Milan–San Remo with only Raymond Poulidor of the 232 starters for company, lapped all the domestic British semi-professionals in London, and rode maybe the hardest race of his life in the Tour of Lombardy.

Roger St Pierre recalled: 'Tom put up the fight of a lifetime, attacking, attacking, attacking as the race wound round the shores of Lake Maggiore, basking in the October sunshine. Gianni Motta remained in the lead. Tom weathered the last of the hard climbs. Only the final, nearly flat, run back to Como remained. But he had shot his bolt and could no longer hold on to his rival's wheel.

'What purgatory he must have gone through in those tantalising few miles as rider after rider went past him. His tired legs just could not respond any longer.

'Only courage kept him going. When I finally spotted him plodding slowly down the last half-mile to the line, he looked terrible. His face was drawn, fatigue oozing out of every line. His eyes looked lifeless. He was completely, utterly spent. I helped him to the changing rooms and even had to untie his shoelaces for him. He was quivering with fatigue, his eyes red-rimmed and unable to focus. Yet, half an hour later he was the same old Tom, laughing and joking and trying to talk me into extending my holiday so that I could accompany him to a race in central Italy.'

In many ways, the world championship in 1965 was the beginning of his end. Sloshing through the rain in San Sebastian in northern Spain, he broke away with the German Rudi Altig. Both men had been badly ill at the start of the year.

Simpson was at the front all day, and the rest were worn away until only Altig remained. They talked in the last mile, saying afterwards that they had resolved to have a straight sprint for the line (an odd announcement: surely you would only discuss something *other* than a straight sprint?). And Simpson won by a couple of lengths. It was and is the only time this century a Briton was world professional road champion.

'Normally,' said one report, 'Altig would have been a clear favourite with his scorching sprint, but Tom's will to win conquered.'

But again things went wrong. Simpson anticipated big earnings. World champions were worth more then, when there were more criteriums in which to show off their rainbow jerseys. The contracts came in, but that winter Simpson broke his leg skiing, which dismissed his chances for the following season. It put him under pressure. He had committed himself to building a block of flats as an investment in Ghent and to building holiday homes in Corsica. Potentially, his outgoings were high.

'I think he got used to having the money,' said Alec Taylor, his manager in the 1967 Tour. 'He wanted to win the Tour this year, he really wanted that. It was his make-or-break year, you know? I think he knew he could never be world champion again, so he had to win the Tour.'

He was tied to Peugeot as his sponsor, which refused to release him from his contract to join teams making better offers. Finally Peugeot told him he would be out of that year's Tour unless he signed for the following year as well. Since the Tour meant so much — everything — to a rider's career, he was trapped.

It was, says writer Geoffrey Nicholson, his salvation that he could ride in 1967 for Britain and not for Peugeot. He wanted to earn £50,000, which he could do from the Tour and a few other races, and retire. He ordered a Mercedes from a garage in Ghent, drove with his wife Helen to the station, and caught the train to Paris.

Helen said: 'He went to the Tour with, in his head, that he was going to win the Tour that year. When I said goodbye to him at the station in Ghent, those were his very last words: to win the Tour that year.'

On July 13, 1967, the race was in Marseille. The 103 riders left were to ride 100 miles north to Mont Ventoux, an arid mountain shaped like the dome of St Paul's. They would turn up the mountain, ride 10 miles averaging one-in-ten and emerge on the shelterless grey stone of the summit. Then all that was left was to race down the other side to see who would be first into Carpentras.

It was already hot. Tar was running down the road.

The organisers, the newspapers *Parisien Libéré* and *L'Equipe*, liked Mont Ventoux. It gave drama to contrast with the flat, unexciting stages down the west coast. In earlier races there had been protests about riding in such heat. Jean Mallejac and the Belgian van Genechten had collapsed on the Ventoux in earlier races. Simpson himself asked the French journalist Jean Leulliot whether trees had been planted on the parched country which led to the summit. But nobody claimed the volcano should be dropped.

Vin Denson recalled: 'He said he hated crickets. He had this pet hate for crickets. And around Carpentras, Orange, all that area of central France, where the heat and air seemed so dry, the noise from the crickets was unbelievable.

Although we were talking and chatting, and there was the noise from the cars and motorcycles, you could always hear the crickets. And he used to say "I hate those bastards, I really hate them." And I think it was more the hate for the dry type of mountain, the lack of oxygen, that lack of air he hated.'

Sixteen kilometres before Carpentras on the first run through, the doorless white car of the British team went ahead to the feeding zone. Crowds had gathered and thickened steadily.

Simpson had not slept well and had been pushed by his team-mates to save energy for the climb. He was third in the snaking line for food bags. He took both hands off his handlebars, grabbed the bag and ferried the contents to his jersey pockets. Alec Taylor repeated the procedure with the rest of the team, then drove to the back of the bunch in a race with the other team cars. He arrived as the race approached Bedoin at the foot of the climb to the summit of Mont Ventoux (1,895m).

Alan Gayfer considered: 'There's no question that Tom was afraid of the Ventoux. Everybody is afraid of the Ventoux. Eddy Merckx himself is afraid of the Ventoux. They know that the Ventoux is an extremely tough mountain to climb; that's *why* they climb it.'

Thirty thousand spectators were estimated to have gathered on the ascent where, at the Chalet Reynard, Bernard Bebière and Roger Viau remember their café thermometer bursting at 54 degrees Celsius.

At the front were Raymond Poulidor and the Spanish climber Julio Jimenez. Both nurtured much the same thought as Simpson. They were still leading near the summit, joined by the Italian Felice Gimondi. Just over 5km from the top, they passed the Chalet Reynard and its burst thermometer. The road was melting badly.

Two riders passed after Gimondi, and then Simpson. He was followed by the Frenchman Lucien Aimar, who had dropped behind by a hundred metres or so. Now, as Simpson was riding unsteadily out of the shade, Aimar was about to catch him again. The team car reached Simpson at that very moment.

Mechanic Harry Hall recalls: 'As we got to him, he was losing ground on this group. So I obviously thought he had taken on more than he could manage.'

Simpson weakened suddenly and Aimar passed him, followed by four others. He kept pedalling for a mile in the heat. The landscape was lunar grey. There was no vegetation. And then he started to wobble.

Harry Hall: 'His riding became jerky. He lost his flow. He rode criss-crossing across the climb. And then he rode to the left-hand side of the road, and there's quite a sheer drop. If you go over, you don't stop on one of those things. He did this a couple of times and I was ready to jump out of the car when he swung back and he hit the bank on the right-hand side. He tried to turn the bike and he got in the rough stuff at the side. His speed had dropped and he fell over against the bank, on his right-hand shoulder. I remember well, I said: "That's it, Tom. That's it for you!", and I undid his toestraps. And at this point he burst into "No, no!" — he wouldn't have that. "Get me up, get me up!"

'So he was quite coherent. He said "I want to go on. Get me up, get me straight!"'

Taylor was on the other side.

'For God's sake concentrate,' he said, and the wobbling stopped. Simpson shouted for Hall to retighten the toestraps and he pressed on for another 300 metres, his tyres splashing in tar, his head characteristically tilted to one shoulder. His white jersey with its two Union Jacks was stretched across his narrow back. His eyes stared lack-lustre into the tar.

A photographer from the American UPI agency took a picture of him at that moment and realised what he was seeing. Without waiting for confirmation, he drove straight on to the finish and wired back a picture with the message that Simpson was dead. Asked later how he could be so confident tragedy would follow, he said: 'I saw when I went past him; death was in his face.'

For a moment his rhythm returned. But a kilometre from the summit, Simpson began to weave seriously, and he rode to a stop. He collapsed, still strapped to his bike, onto the road.

Harry Hall ran to him again.

'I'm trying to get him off his bike and I remember saying to Ken [Ryall, the other mechanic], "Get his hands off the bars." Because I'd got my body underneath his, to lift him off, to put him on my back in other words, and his hands were still on the bars. And Ken had to peel his fingers to release the bars, and the bike then just fell down.'

Taylor said afterwards that there was no reason to suspect he was suffering from anything more than effort and heat. He reasoned the descent would revive him, and his worry was not that Simpson was dying, which he did not realise, but that he would take too many risks to catch up lost time. There was scarcely a mile to the summit.

The white Peugeot lay neglected by the roadside as they laid Simpson's head on the white sticky road. Dr Dumas, alerted by the race radio, was alongside. Hall stopped his mouth-to-mouth resuscitation, and Dumas and his assistant Macorig put Simpson's head into a portable oxygen mask. They massaged his heart until a police helicopter arrived to whisk him away. Macorig and Nurse Daumas continued the massage on their way to the central hospital at Avignon. But Simpson was evidently already dead.

'He looked absolutely dreadful,' Hall said. 'There was no sign of what you would call life in him at that point, although you never know. He wasn't breathing.'

Eerily, Simpson had said in a BBC radio interview some time earlier: 'Your bottom might be sore, your legs aching, your back is aching from bending over the handlebars. You're very often hungry. All the organs just tend to cease to work. When a rider makes big efforts, and his body isn't in tune to do those efforts, he has a temporary blackout. You could get off, but you have to use your courage and fight it off.'

Many more minutes were to pass before Denson reached the point of the drama, where a growing crowd surrounded Simpson.

'I noticed the cars there and the ambulance, all confusion. And suddenly to my horror I realised it was Tom lying down there.'

Alarmed but convinced that Simpson had merely overdone it, and knowing the doctors were there, Denson rode on towards Carpentras. There, he did what all the minor riders did — crossed the line, turned in the road, and cycled to his hotel.

He recalled what happened next.

'I'd taken my bike to have some work to be done, and the mechanic turned to me and he said "He's dead. I'm certain he's dead."

'And I said "No, no, it's not possible, Harry." And Harry said "Well, he's been taken to hospital. We can hope for the best but I'm certain he's dead." And that knocked me personally and I started to think there was a possibility that he could have been dead. And as we went in for the meal, Alec Taylor pulled me to one side and he said "We've had positive news from the hospital — he's been announced dead on arrival at the hospital." And although I was a grown man, I remember being almost hysterical in tears. I felt as if something of me had died when Tom died.'

The two were friends. They and their wives planned to holiday together later that summer. In their room, the team voted whether to continue. Denson was for stopping, for going to the funeral, but he went along with the rest.

Taylor was asked to race headquarters in Carpentras to explain what had happened. As he got back into the team car, he tuned away from Radio Tour and let the receiver wander across as many of Europe's radio stations as it could pick up. In the languages of the world, he said, he could hear Simpson's name in news bulletins.

'It was a pretty dreadful time.'

Helen Simpson was on holiday in Corsica with her parents. On July 13 she was on the beach with Blanche Leulliot, the wife of French journalist Jean

Leulliot. They were listening to the radio. Helen picked up that Simpson had fallen, but Blanche Leulliot sensed it was rather more urgent. She rang her husband at race headquarters and her face grew grimmer as the conversation progressed. As she placed the handpiece back on the cradle, she told Helen Simpson's father, and it was from him that Helen Simpson heard her husband had died.

Next day, Bastille Day, riders walked to Denson, often weeping, and shook hands in sympathy. One, Jean Stablinksi, said Denson should win that day's journey into Sête as a tribute.

As it turned out it was Barry Hoban who won.

'We were all riding at the front, and the next thing I looked round and there was no one there. To this day, I don't know how far I rode on my own. I could tell you every inch of the Ghent–Wevelgem that I won, but I can't tell you much about that.'

Denson was hidden among the mass of riders.

'I was riding in a complete trance,' he said. 'I was crying, and whenever I saw another English jersey, I kept looking and thinking it was Tom again. And I kept listening and hearing Tom's voice all the time.'

It took more than a month for the Tour de France authorities to confirm what the *Daily Mail* had already reported — that Simpson had taken drugs. The autopsy blamed sunstroke and oxygen starvation. There were drugs and alcohol in his body and three pill tubes in the pockets of his jersey.

The drugs, said the delayed official report, had allowed him 'to pass the limit of his endurance and so fall victim to excessive exhaustion.'

The police said Simpson was put aboard the helicopter at 4.40pm and arrived at the Sainte-Marthe hospital at 5.15. His death was announced to the press room at 5.40 by the race's co-organiser, Felix Lévitan. Burial permission was refused.

Two of the tubes in Simpson's clothing were empty. A third contained a few of two kinds of tablets. They were Stenamina and Tonedrin, made respectively by the Pepitit company of Milan and Laboratoires Grimault of Paris. Searches of the team's baggage at Sête revealed more drugs in Simpson's luggage.

It started the biggest clean-up campaign that any sport has ever known. It still hasn't entirely succeeded.

Barry Hoban said, 25 years afterwards: 'A lot of people — the medical profession included — were not aware of the problems that are apparent today. They were just not aware of them. Tom was looking after himself in a way that a lot of people were looking after themselves. Maybe you could accuse us, and I was part of that generation, of being ill-advised, but we were ill-advised by the medical profession from the knowledge that they had then.

'There wasn't a drug problem in those days. Perhaps happy Flower People. There wasn't a problem that was apparent to the medical profession. Hence the reason why certain habits were formed …

'He was racing under conditions that were apparent to everyone racing at that time.'

Against that you have to balance the conclusion that the problems were in fact very well known indeed, since not only had cycling begun drug testing but the drugs themselves were specifically banned to sportsmen by French law 65,412.

But Colin Lewis, who shared a room with Simpson in that Tour, said: 'He had that much class and ability that he could have done it on a glass of water.'

So many came to Simpson's funeral at Harworth that the service was relayed to those who stood outside in the rain. There were current champions, ancient champions, and ordinary clubfolk. His club in Ghent wrote these words: 'Tom, you came to Flanders as a small, unknown racing cyclist. You won the hearts of all Flemish cycle fans in a very short time. Your charm, your everlasting smile, were two of your secrets. Your fighter's temperament and your great heart made us consider you to be a real Flandrian, one of our own people. That great heart came to a stop for ever on the pitiless Ventoux in that cruel struggle for life …

'Fate struck hard and pitilessly. It snatched you away for ever. We will miss you dearly. Farewell, good friend.'

Alan Gayfer began a public subscription for a stained-glass window to Simpson's memory, and then, when the cost became prohibitive, for a memorial on Mont Ventoux.

It's there now, and the Tour de France lays a wreath when it passes. But when it goes that way these days, it's always in late afternoon. The sun is cooler then.

4 BRIAN ROBINSON (1930–)

Simpson was merely the most celebrated of those who crossed the Channel to try racing abroad. But he wasn't the first. Nobody knows who was. But Simpson had at least a role model in Brian Robinson, who in turn could look to Charles Holland.

Robinson is a quiet and unassuming man. In Mirfield, an uphill sort of place near Huddersfield in West Yorkshire, Robinson is a name more linked to building than biking. But the younger brother, as well as being a builder, has done a bit of cycling as well. He is the first Briton to win a stage of the Tour de France.

Come into town from the motorway end and you drop down a gentle hillside on a secondary road, Stocks Bank Road, which is busy enough but not unkind to cyclists. On the left, before the bottom, is Robinson's house. I offered a time to meet him and he suggested half an hour later — 'I should be up from the table by then,' he said.

Brian Robinson by no means takes life in carpet slippers and cardigans, but he knows now what life and its pleasures can mean. He's done the hard bit.

To put him in context, you have to go back to that other pioneer, Charles Holland. Look up *Cycling* for December 1989 and you'll find the announcement of his death at 81.

Charles Holland was the first Briton to ride the Tour de France. Somebody had to be the first, but what makes Holland's participation all the more remarkable is that the very magazine which detailed his life with pride in 1989 saw fit to write only a few paragraphs a week in the 1930s of the world's greatest bike race. Men with strange names competed in faraway lands of which we knew little, and *Cycling* wasn't about to tell us much more.

The pioneering Tour was in 1937, and Holland rode with Bill Burl and a French-Canadian called Pierre Gachon, as a British Empire team. It wasn't a great success. Gachon didn't finish the first day, and Burl was so far behind in the next stage that the organisers threw him out. It left Holland as the lone representative of an empire on which the sun still never set.

He rode for 2,000 miles until he became stranded by the roadside like a simple clubman who's run out of puncture patches. Worse, his pump — riders still carried pumps — was broken.

He and the others had set out to ride 204 miles in three sections to Luchon. The route crossed five Pyrénéan cols. Just before the peak of the col de Port, Holland punctured when he was 30 metres behind the leaders. He changed his tyre and pressed the pump to its valve. But it was a stinking hot day and the sun had warped the washer. There was no help from the team cars and, as the rest of the race struggled by him, Holland fought to get his spare tyre to half-pressure. He despaired of getting it fully blown, climbed on and rode on looking for a spectator with a pump. But scarcely had he got the tyre inflated than he punctured twice more on the descent. And he had no more spares. It caused a frisson of interest.

'A crowd of peasants had gathered around me, but they couldn't help me. A priest brought me a bottle of beer, and although it quenched my thirst it got me no further. After I had given up hope, a tourist came along and gave me a tubular touring tyre. I put it on, and in the excitement the rod of the pump broke. We blew the tyre hard with another pump but the tyre fitted so loosely on the rim that it came off with the fingers and so was unsafe. Another tyre was found which fitted a little better, and I again set off, but I had by then given up hope. When I arrived at the control, where we were to receive food and drink, the officials had gone. I took my number off and definitely retired.'

A carload of Belgian journalists tried to dissuade him, but his race was over. He makes not even a passing mention in books on the Tour de France.

Eighteen years after Charles Holland, Britain entered a team of 10 in 1955. George Pearson, the editor of *Cycling*, forecast they would achieve a place in the top 12. How come such a change in fortunes?

To realise that, you have to marvel at the naiveté of the boy of 13 who joined the Huddersfield Road Club alongside his father and his brother Des. He wasn't allowed to race until he was 18, a rule of his father's, and the frustrated young Robinson spent his time reading *But et Club*, *Miroir Sprint* — Continental magazines which post-war cyclists passed around as their sons might swap *Mayfair* and *Penthouse*. They were different days.

Des was three years older, and a lot of people thought he was better than Brian as an amateur and might even have become a better professional. But Des had a persistent sinus problem and retired from racing in 1956 to move to

Teesside, as a draughtsman at Wilton, in the hope that exchanging the heavy woollen district for the air of the North Yorkshire coast would help.

Brother Brian said: 'I wanted to road-race, which at the time was restricted to old wartime airfields and parks, and I rode a lot at Sutton Park in Birmingham. I would ride to Sheffield or Birmingham, getting up at six, and we would have to leave the park at 9.30am because the public would want to use it.'

Training amounted to as many miles as possible, weight training in the garage, some roller riding, and mammoth bashes to Romney Marsh in Kent and back in four days.

He made steady progress, fifth in the National Cyclists' Union road championship and third in the hillclimb championship in 1950, then he was equal seventh in the Isle of Man International in 1951. In those days we still had an army that marched around a lot, and in 1952, Olympic year, Robinson was doing compulsory service in the King's Own Yorkshire Light Infantry. It could have been worse. The army, with more men than it knew what to do with, had a knack of putting like spirits together in the hope of winning inter-service and even national championships.

Robinson's squad might have amounted to a national team.

'I found myself in an ace unit of Procter, Willmott, Pusey, Mitchell and Kirton, the finest bunch of soldiers any cyclist would want to see in his billet.'

In the same year he made his first overseas trip, to the Route de France, the amateur version of the Tour. Sure enough, in a composite of NCU and army riders, Robinson, Peter Procter, Bernard Pusey and Les Willmott were all on the army side. The NCU had Brian Haskell, Robinson's brother Des, Dick Henly and Alan Ashmore.

'We were raw amateurs with no experience and no equipment,' he said.

He was fifth with three days to go, then he found the Pyrénées for the first time and fell to 40th. Procter, the revelation, was 15th, Haskell 33rd, Des Robinson 55th and Pusey 60th. Henly and Ashmore had crashed and left the race.

Robinson recalled: 'I never did get any prize money. We were thrown in the deep end. I had never seen mountains like that before. It was a big learning session.'

There were no professionals in Britain then, so he turned independent, or semi-professional, next year for a bike shop called Ellis-Briggs. The team's main rider, Ken Russell, had won the Tour of Britain in 1952. Next year Robinson finished second and began attracting big attention.

The cycle trade in England had scarcely changed from the boom years of the 1930s, with antiquated production lines and selling methods which had survived the war with more attention from the Luftwaffe than from their own management. There was an outdoor boom in the 1950s, but nothing compared with what had followed the first war. Worse, it was a craving for the outdoors that could be fed by the car and by public bus, both of which were now being made in larger numbers to satisfy servicemen who'd learned to drive during the war.

Bike factories were in a sorry state and set about competing as much with each other as they did with the car makers. At first they decided it was unwise and agreed among themselves to reduce their publicity expenditure — but then the biggest began sponsoring professional teams. They were to be not simply part-timers but men who could live and ride permanently on the Continent, where they would be pioneers, and a handful of women hired for their record-breaking capacities.

Robinson talked to BSA and Hercules about a pro contract for 1955. It wasn't straightforward.

'Syd Cozens, who represented BSA, said I had to sign there and then or the deal was off. I told him I would probably sign, but next day Hercules put in a better offer so I signed for them. By the end of the week BSA had folded. Yet, lo and behold, Cozens became team manager for Hercules. He was a bandit.'

Other teams fell short of the Continental ideal, but Hercules longed for the Tour de France. In Robinson, Bernard Pusey, Dennis Talbot, Freddy Krebs, Clive Parker, Ken Joy (soon replaced by Bob Maitland), Arthur Ilsley, Derek Buttle and Dave Bedwell, they had experience.

Robinson gave up work, trained 80 miles daily before lunch, and pored over the tiny amount of advice then available for serious athletes. Hercules went to the south of France to train, then returned to take first four in the South Elmsall Spring Classic.

Robinson was fourth in the Tour of Calvados, Tony Hoar won a stage of the Tour of Holland and came second in another. Robinson was fourth in Flèche Wallonne.

The Tour de France was for national teams, which for Britain meant Hercules.

Robinson recalled: 'Those first Tours were like a small club; you were always up against the same riders. We were like racing cars competing against Concorde. I rode like an amateur, attacking three or four times instead of making one big, powerful effort. Three or four years into pro cycling you learn your métier. You become craftier and learn how to read a race.'

Bedwell and Wood were out by the third stage, and by halfway only Robinson and Hoar were left. Robinson finished 29th, the first Englishman to finish. He said he felt like one of a number of green bottles hanging from a wall; except for two, they all fell. Hoar came last but became a celebrity in demand for criteriums.

'It was a great feeling to finish the Tour, a lifetime's ambition realised. You are out of the amateur status then. You have grown up.'

Next year was relatively uneventful, but 1957 was spectacular for a minnow. The season was barely weeks old when he achieved his first professional win, in the GP de Nice. Bobet was second at 50 seconds.

'The start was absolute panic. Just imagine 250 riders all struggling to get a good place when the flag was dropped. From the start until Nice was reached, I concentrated on staying on the bike, which was difficult at times owing to the very narrow roads and every rider pushing his way to the front.'

He knew the climb out of Nice, the Turbie, and got to the front for the first time. The climb is 15km long and by the top there were 50 in the first group.

'I was romping up the hill. I must have found one of those days when you just can't feel the pedals. Over the top we turned down a tricky little descent and at the bottom six of us found ourselves well clear of the bunch and our reaction was immediate and we started working well together. I surveyed our chances and thought we were well off as Mayzencq, my team-mate, was one of the ace climbers in the Tour and I expected him to take his leave up one of the hills.'

The last climb was the Mont de Mule, a hard eight kilometres. Robinson had never ridden it without being shot off, including two days previously in Genoa–Nice.

'All this time I had been expecting Meyzencq to attack somewhere on the climb, so I thought if I can escape at the bottom of the hill, I can possibly stay with Meyzencq when he comes by. So I dropped back a few yards and took a flyer. Much to my surprise, the only thing I had done was get rid of my own team-mate!

'I again hung back a few yards and snicked in a higher gear. I was off before they could do anything about it. I had a mile to go to the top and when I got there I had 25 seconds. I had 20km to go. Could I do it? In the early season one is never sure of just how good one's form is, but neither are the other riders, so it balances out. It was mostly downhill, so what could I lose if I got caught? I thought of all the things that could happen, like punctures, dogs in the road, going the wrong way and so on, but in the end I was in sight of the banner, and I was very happy to cross that line and chalk up my first Number One.

'At last I had got the sash, the flowers and the pretty girl to embrace, too.'

With a note of bitterness at the way those who had put factory money into bike teams had then lost their jobs, Robinson added that it was 'a reminder to some members of the British cycle industry who think that British cyclists haven't got what it takes.'

Then he finished third in Milan–San Remo, behind Miguel Poblet of Spain and the Belgian Fred De Bruyne, who went on to become a television commentator and, later, team manager and public relations chief to Peter Post. Riding Milan–San Remo was no more straightforward than turning professional had been.

'My manager Raymond Louviot had a tie-up in the cycle trade with Poblet. He told me that if Poblet was anywhere near me, it was my job to get him over the line first. I buggered off up a hill and then my manager came up and told me "Remember what I told you." Poblet won, I was third. That is my biggest regret. If I had won, I would have been made for life.'

Winning a Tour stage didn't make him for life. In other lands, in Belgium or France, he might have become enough of a celebrity to open a garage or a bar and retire, but fame counted for little in Britain. He didn't even finish the Tour, a victim of food poisoning, but at least he had made history if not money by winning the seventh stage. Although he might have preferred to win in different circumstances.

The race had covered only 50 of the 170km when Robinson attacked and took with him the Frenchman Jean Dotto and Italy's Padovan. It was a break of no importance, the cats sniffing haughtily as the mice played before them, but there are days when a man can make a name, however lowly, and this was Robinson's. He shook off Dotto but couldn't get rid of Padovan.

'He hadn't a smell of winning. It was a long uphill finish and I put my head down and went.' He clicked down from 52 ˘ 14 to 16 and kept going. Padovan went left. And as Robinson came by on the right, Padovan pushed him into the gutter and into the crowd, twice..

The judges sympathised and Padovan's win went to Robinson instead. A Briton had won for the first time.

'I was greatly elated at my stage win, not just because it was a first for Britain or Brian Robinson but because I knew I would be sure of a good contract for the following year.'

In 1959 he benefited again from what the French call a fallen bottle — the inconsequential attack. This time he had been hit badly on the 14th stage, diving from ninth overall to being so far back that at first he was eliminated. The judges put him back in the race, and by stage 20 he had won his second stage, 20-06 or seven miles ahead of the next finisher.

Robinson was astute enough to see the parallels with the previous win. And this time he fitted light, 36-spoke wheels he'd bought in Italy and fitted them with 180g tubulars intended for the time-trial.

Dotto came with him again on the climb of the Echallon, but he dropped off on the descent, expecting the bunch to catch both of them. It never did.

Robinson plugged on, and in another re-run of the first victory Padovan was again second.

One measure of how different those days were came in 1957. Look up *Cycling* for January 17 and you'll find a little announcement that he arranged to appear in its pages. It said:

'Brian Robinson, who began his brilliant 1956 stage-racing saga with seventh place in the Tour of Spain, has been asked by the organisers of the race to arrange four British professionals to join him in forming a mixed Portuguese–British team in this year's Tour ... Riders interested in competing, or would-be professionals, should contact Brian Robinson as soon as possible at 96 Stocks Bank Road, Mirfield, Yorkshire.'

It's hard to imagine Gianni Bugno or Eddy Merckx doing the same.

5 WIM VAN EST (1923–)

It took me two days to ride from Peter Post (see Chapter 2) to Wim van Est, from the Dutch midlands to the southern border. Anyone half-fit could do it in less, but I wanted to stick to byways and take it easy, and there was also a headwind and a nagging memory of my night on the ferry.

I'd showered and dropped on to the bed. For a while, bliss, I had the cabin to myself; the ship was far from full. But the economical Dutch had booked in someone else rather than soil two cabins, and an hour later he arrived, coughing, sneezing and hoping his cold would go by the time he'd driven to Sweden.

My nose ran and my legs turned leaden as I rode south. I booked into a hotel run by René Pijnen, an old six-day rider I never managed to meet despite conversations in phone boxes, and set off again in the evening for St Willebrord, the village that played host to the Tour de France in 1978 (the cost having been whipped up by holding raffles and other fund-raisers). I was looking for Hazelaarstraat, in the dark, and I called across to builders working by lamplight. I think they were grateful for a rest. There followed a conference in wellingtons and heavy dialect. Nobody quite knew the road.

'Where van Est lives, isn't it?' I heard them saying.

'*Precies!*' I said.

'Then why didn't you say so in the first place?' chided the Head Wellington. 'Everyone knows where *he* lives.'

St Willebrord is between Roosendaal and Breda in Noord-Brabant, where the people are shorter and darker than in the north. Stubborn, too, because they call their village not St Willebrord but 't Heike, pronounced like Tizer but with a 'k'. Something to do with people who ought to know better changing the name of a village that the locals wanted left alone.

The local club, Willebrord Wil Vooruit ('Up With Willebrord'), has produced one world champion, three Yellow Jerseys, three Green Jerseys, 11 Tour de France stage winners, several Dutch champions, an Olympic gold medallist and rather more besides. It has a thick and coloured book, a club history, which another member, Rini Wagtmans, gave me next morning with some pride — a club history with more success than many an entire nation.

I was late and van Est came to the door in his slippers, blinking into the street lights. It was a neat house in small bricks, the front garden full of the shrubs that the Dutch love. Inside, an old pal was watching football on television.

Wim van Est is the shape of a barrel. He was when he was racing and he is now. Ask him to a party and everyone would have a whale of a time. He laughs, he drinks, he smokes (without inhaling), and he bangs on the table and grabs your arm as he tells you a story. He loves telling stories.

Wim van Est is a man who thinks life is great fun. And so would you, if you'd been the first Dutchman to wear the Yellow Jersey (after the stage from Agen to Dax in 1951), the first Dutchman to take the pink Giro jersey (1953), and the first to win the Tour of Flanders (also 1953). The Dutch call him Iron Bill, or the *tempobeul*, or speed-bully. *Beul*, incidentally, can also mean hangman or torturer, which gives you an idea of how the old boy rode. And if you had won Bordeaux–Paris three times, you too would be happy. Even working for 18 years on the railways afterwards can't take the edge off that.

We drank coffee and he kept half an eye on the football.

'One day as a boy, I remember standing watching a race in St Willebrord, astonished that they couldn't go any faster. I told a couple of friends and they suggested I have a go myself, then. I had an ordinary race bike and I started training, and it went really well.

'We had these training races with a coal lorry as the service car. I was always up front with Marijn Valentijn and we gave it so much gas that the back of the lorry was full of riders who'd given up. At the end they got off as black as miners from the coaldust. And that's when I started entering proper races.

'We never had any money, so we had to be clever. We used to have a trick to get a drink while we were out training. We'd get to a shop and one of us would fall off and lie in the gutter.

'Well, naturally, people used to come out of the shop to see what had happened. "An accident, eh?" And there would be my mate lying in the gutter. "Oh, I'm not too bad," he used to say, "but I wouldn't half mind a drink." And then someone would go and get a bottle of something and he'd take a few mouthfuls and then further up the road he'd share what was left with the rest of us.'

And he laughed again and grabbed my arm. His accent got thicker the more excited he became.

'Riders today, they'd go mad if they had to do what we did. We thought it was great if we got a lift on a lorry to a race in Zeeland [40 miles away]. We used to sit on a load of planks on the back. No bother. And then we'd try to find a farmer's shed to sleep in, and roll up in the hay, and in the morning we made sure we were up before the farmer so that we could pinch the eggs from under the hens for breakfast.

'And I remember, in the Dutch club championship, I was away with Wout Wagtmans. We were getting to the finish when, 500 metres before the line, he saw this little children's bike in the crowd. So he jumped off, grabbed this kiddy-bike, and finished the race on it. Laugh? I'd never seen anything so funny in my life. Unfortunately the judges didn't see it the same way and they disqualified both of us, even though we were eight minutes clear.'

On another occasion, a Belgian team-mate spotted a little box of pills in van Est's team car. He sidled up to the Dutchman and asked whether taking them would get him through Bordeaux–Paris.

'I'm looking for something really strong,' said the Belgian.

'Exactly what you want,' van Est said confidentially, took the box out of the team car and gave it to him. 'Take them a quarter of an hour before the start.'

The Belgian promised faithfully to return the favour and rode to the start. Two kilometres later, he had to climb off his bike.

'They were flints for the team manager's lighter!' van Est roared.

'I started as a pro for nothing. Just my shorts and a jersey. Nothing else. But then in '49, I rode the Tour of Holland and I won a stage in that against tough opposition, from Apeldoorn to Helmond. A lot of Belgians. But the first day … I was put into a team, see? We just had a sponsor for a week. We got a jersey and they paid for your meals and your bed. No bonuses, see, because that would have cost too much.

'And I had to do all the work. They'd shout "Wim, I've punctured … wait!" And over the Afsluitdijk [the windy 29-kilometre dam across the old Zuider Zee], we used to have spare tyres round our shoulders, and when they punctured they used to hang on for a tow on the tyre and I had to pull the blokes back to the bunch. Man, man, man!

'In the first day, I lost 26 minutes — in a stage of 160km.'

The astonishing thing is that he still finished ninth overall.

Holland had a pro race on Saturday and another on Sunday. van Est, who could ride to the border in an hour, managed a criterium a day in Belgium as well.

'I was the first real star we had in Holland, I suppose. On the road, anyway. I mean, we had Gerrit Schulte, Kees Pellenaars, van Vliet and Derksen on the track, but …

'Anyway, in 1949 I got a contract to ride the Grand Prix des Nations, because I'd won a time-trial in the Tour of Holland in front of Koblet and good timetriallists, and good Belgians. And I could have won that, too, but I went wrong. I'd never been to France. And I went on the train to Paris, and you had to take a carnet, a little book, for the bike, for the customs. Everything, spare wheels, everything, had to be in the book. And I didn't understand a word of French. *Niks!*

'And there was this Frenchman, great big moustache, and he was talking French and I was speaking Dutch and, *ja*, "*Parlez français!*" and I was shaking my head, "*Non, non,*" and he couldn't explain and I couldn't understand and anyway, eventually I got away, after an hour.

'And so then I had to get a hotel. All I had was a card from the manager, Boulevard Magenta, Hôtel d'Angleterre, near the Gare du Nord. I'll take a taxi. And there was this other Frenchman saying "*Pas bicyclette, pas bicyclette*", and I was saying "*Ja, ja, bicyclette*" and we got it all taken to bits and I shoved it up in the front with the meter, and we were driving and driving and driving. Eiffel Tower, Place Pigalle, Place de Napoléon, the Sacré Cœur … and then the Eiffel Tower again.

'I said, "We've already been by here! *Allez*, hotel, hotel!" And he was saying, "*Piano, piano! Doucement!*" And by then I was getting really angry and I was banging on the window and shouting, "*Godverdomme*, hotel!" I was in that taxi for an hour and a half, *godverdomme!*

'And when I got there, there was the *garçon*, with a moustache and a blue apron, and I took the bike upstairs to my room. I mean, it was no chic hotel — just bare floors and old furniture. Well! By five o'clock the cleaning lady was complaining to the *patron* because the bike was dirty — because the previous day I'd won a race in Belgium and it had been raining all day.

'My leather saddle was soaked, my shoes were wet through, and so he said, the *patron*, "Let's take them down to the boiler room, away from the room." And that was fine.

'Next morning — the race was in the afternoon — I thought I'd go out training. There was nothing happening in Paris. No cars, nothing, before 11am. So I put my tracksuit on and I went down to the boiler room, and I just about fell over with shock.

'He'd put my shoes on the top of the stove and leaned my bike against it as well. And, *verdorie*, the saddle was about five inches long. Dried up. All crumpled up from drying out. And my shoes would have fitted a five-year-old. I didn't dare race. I thought I'd have to go back to the station.'

And if it hadn't been for a chance meeting with a handful of Belgian reporters such as Karel Steyaert [who wrote as Wim van Wijnendaele], he probably would have. As luck would have it, the writers scoured Paris and produced a pair of secondhand shoes and a bike with one brake. van Est rode the Grand Prix des Nations and after 145km came second by 13 seconds … after being misdirected at the entrance to the track at the Parc des Princes.

'*Jongen*, those were unbelievable times!'

The journey, though, was nothing compared with travelling to Italy, sleeping two nights in the luggage rack as the train spent three days crossing France.

In 1950 he won Bordeaux–Paris for the first time and in 1952 for the second time. Legend has it that he was after the record, but in fact he was riding simply as a contractual obligation to his sponsor, Maurice Garin, the first winner of the Tour de France, who was paying him 16,000 old French francs a month.

Even that wasn't a lot. He discovered that Ferdy Kübler was getting 10,000 Swiss francs — which, as the old rider Georges Ronsse pointed out to him, meant he could sell Bordeaux–Paris to Kübler, who'd then get his bonus. van Est would forego first place, get nothing from Garin but collect from Kübler, ending up better off than if he had won in the first place. The only problem was that Kübler never paid up.

On another occasion, the organisers of the Acht van Chaam, Holland's oldest criterium, offered him 750 guilders to take part and make a race of it. He was delighted until he read two days later that Rik van Looy was on 6,000 guilders just to start.

'van Looy got off his bike after a couple of kilometres and went home.'

In 1951, 12 days into the Tour de France, van Est became the first Dutchman to win the Yellow Jersey. And being van Est, it didn't happen without a curious story.

'That day, I was away with a group of 13, 14 riders. And there was a really fast rider with us, Caput, the Frenchman. Good sprinter. He attacked a kilometre from the line but we got him back. But when we got to the track, it was an old ash track, a horse-racing track.

'Well, on a track like that, I was unbeatable. I raced on that sort of finish so often. Coppi, Kübler … I was unbeatable. And I won and I took the yellow jersey.'

There was an enormous party in the Dutch team of riders, managers and journalists. Few stayed sober in St Willebrord. But then came the craziest of comic tragedies.

Next day there were several cols. The Tourmalet was one, and then the Aubisque, between Dax and Tarbes. van Est was never a climber, but he had the jersey to defend and he was riding well.

'There were nine or ten men away and we were gritting our teeth to get them back, and then in the first bend of the descent there were just Ockers and Coppi, a few hundred metres in front of us.

'Well, that first bend was wet, slippery from the snow. And there were sharp stones on the road that the cars had kicked up and my front wheel hit them and I went over.

'Well, there was a drop of 20 metres. They've built a barrier round it now, but then there was nothing to stop you going over. I fell 20 metres, rolling and rolling and rolling. My feet had come out of the straps, my bike had disappeared, and there was a little flat area, the only one that's there, no bigger than the seat of a chair, and I landed on my backside.

'A metre left or right and I'd have dropped onto solid stone, six or seven hundred metres down. My ankles were all hurt, my elbows were kaput. I was all bruised and shaken up and I didn't know where I was, but nothing was broken.

'I just lay there. And the other riders were going by, I could see. And then right up at the top I could make out my team-mate, Gerrit Peeters, looking down at me.

'"You looked just like a buttercup down there," he told me afterwards — with the yellow jersey on, you know.'

Half the field hadn't realised what had happened. There was a great chase on, the *maillot jaune* having been high up on the climb, and the chasers hammered all the way to Tarbes, and wondered where he'd got to. Hugo Koblet took the new yellow jersey.

Back on the mountain, Kees Pellenaars, the manager, threw a tow rope to him but it was too short. So he lengthened it with the only things he could find.

'They got 40 tubulars, knotted them together, tied them to the tow rope, and threw it down to me. It was all the tyres that Pellenaars had for the team. By the time they'd tugged me up, all the tubs were stretched and they wouldn't stay on the wheels any more! Forty tubs!

'I wanted to get on my bike and start riding again. One of the journalists gave me a flask of cognac, and I was saying "I want to go on, I want to go on." But I couldn't. Pellenaars stopped the whole team. "We'll be back next year," he said.

'It was good publicity, I got home and the whole neighbourhood was out to greet me.

'*Ja, hoor* ... those were crazy days!'

Oh, and a final thought ... A Swiss watch company had its wits about it when it promptly signed van Est for an advertisement. It showed the Dutchman battered from his fall down the mountain. Beneath him was the slogan: 'My heart stopped, but not my Pontiac.'

6 RIK VAN LOOY (1933–)

I was, to be honest, worried about my next appointment. The wind was howling and my nose streaming. There was also the nagging fear that the Emperor of Herentals wasn't going to be easy.

I spent the morning with friends a few villages from van Est, then rode past the abandoned border control at Essen and on into Kalmthout, the first 'real' village in Belgium. Turn right at the end of the village and you ride briefly back into Holland before arriving at Putte (which means 'well'), a village divided by the Dutch–Belgian border and home to two former world champions — Jan Janssen and Hennie Kuiper.

Belgium's quite unlike Holland: the roads are obviously tar laid over cobbles — and sometimes not too successfully — and the villages far less like the Toytown newness of Holland and more in need of a lick of paint.

I'd given up hope of riding to Herentals and caught the train from Antwerp. It was all but snowing when I found a hotel with poky rooms and stained wallpaper at 10pm.

'Just ask for the Bloso centre,' van Looy had said on the phone. 'Everyone will know it. I'll be there for the bike-racing school.'

Bloso is one of those made-up words of initials — physical education and development it means, roughly, and I'd imagined a school playground with traffic cones to mark a course. Instead, in a wood to the north of the town, you start seeing those triangular road signs that contain an exclamation mark.

In most countries, they might mean a factory exit or a ramp. But under these signs are a word you see on warnings only in Belgium. *Wielrenners*, they say. Beware racing cyclists!

If you approach from the north, you ride the cycle path alongside the Poederleesesteenweg. Not far from the turning to Vorselaar, where the old

Belgian champion Daniël Willems lives, you pass the house of one of the smallest big men in the game. His name is Henri van Looy, better known as Rik.

And in the wood, which is why the signs are there, he has passed the last decade running the Vlaamse Wielerschool. It's a white single-storey building between tennis courts and an ice rink. On the door is a sign, 'Doping? Not me!', and beyond it a black-and-white poster-sized photograph of the man himself, his Belgian champion's jersey sweaty as he hauls himself up one of the cobbled hills of the Tour of Flanders. He certainly wasn't on the 53 ˘ 13 gear that he pioneered, but he might well have been on the way to one of his 513 victories.

What you notice about van Looy, apart from how startlingly he looks as he did in his prime, are the hooked nose and the bright, concentrated, darting eyes, dark and incisive. He grins like a Halloween melon and his eyes gleam. But on August 22, 1970, they were duller. Much duller. Because then, on the way back from Valkenswaard in Holland in his Mercedes, Rik van Looy decided suddenly to stop racing.

'I was tired', he says, 'of riding against snot-noses who, even if you took them all together, hadn't managed a fraction of what I'd achieved. And yet sometimes when they'd beaten me, I'd hear them saying "Oh, we gave that old geezer a hard time today." I couldn't take being called granddad. I was too good a rider for that. So above all else, I stopped because of the break of respect. In the last years I was lining up with riders who could have been my son. I had nothing in common with them. They were another generation.

'Physically, I could have gone on. The training was getting harder, but I could still do it. But I couldn't take that disrespect. The big riders, the stars, they were different. They knew what I'd achieved and how difficult it was to do it. You can only know that if you've been in the closing phases of a classic yourself, if you've done it yourself. And these little riders thought they could laugh at me.'

You can't blame van Looy for his pride. He comes from Antwerp, or rather just outside, and there are no prouder people in Belgium. '*Antwerpenaar — en fier op!*' say the car stickers — 'Antwerper, and proud of it'. So far as they're concerned, Brabo the giant who ruled over the entrance to the Schelde river rules still over Belgium (even though his slain body lies now as a statue in the city centre, water instead of blood flowing through the arteries in a severed hand).

And van Looy was too proud to train, despite the 2,000 francs a month that the Garin team was paying him on his reputation as an amateur. Look up the results of the 1953 Giro d'Italia and, if they go far enough down, you'll see van Looy among the last five riders home each day. On one stage they'd begun taking down the grandstands by the time he arrived.

Once he told Pierre Thonon of *La Cité*: 'To start with, I couldn't be bothered and I wasn't fussed about going training. That was fine while I was an amateur. But things changed just a bit when I turned pro!' It was a view sharpened by a drop in his next contract to just 1,600 francs.

The old manager, Lomme Driessens, entered him for the Giro on the promise that the weather was always fine, most of the course flat, and bunches frequently ended the race intact — ideal for a sprinter. Ideal, too, for a man doing national service in the Belgian army. Driessens also told him the Giro was rarely fast.

'Needless to say,' said van Looy, 'the first stage was at 29mph. Every day I finished a bit more behind the last group. On the ninth stage I finished after the judges had gone and after they'd begun dismantling the stands.'

It was a tough lesson. van Looy began training. On his return to Belgium and before returning to the army barracks, he played cat-and-mouse with anyone who dared challenge him. It began at Mechelen, on the border of the French and Dutch-speaking regions, and just carried on. Of the next 25 races, he never finished outside the first five.

From there on he won every classic — more than Merckx, who never won Paris–Tours. The first was Ghent–Wevelgem in 1956, followed by two world championships, five Tour de France stages, 12 Giro stages, 18 Vuelta stages and 12 six-day races on the track.

A Belgian journalist, looking for a new line, called him the Emperor of Herentals, and the name stuck. And Jacques Anquetil once said of him: 'My main rival in the tours wasn't Baldini or Gaul or Poulidor. It was van Looy. I had to match him in the flat stages and even in the mountains, because if I didn't, he would turn up at the time-trials with a 15-minute advantage.'

Rik van Looy was 13 when he started a newspaper round and 15 when he saved and borrowed enough from his parents to buy a secondhand racing bike in 1948. It was stuck in a giant gear. He knocked about with a chap called Julien Vermeulen and went to races with him.

'My admiration for Rik van Steenbergen and Nest Sterckx did the rest. Then one day I entered a race for youngsters in Herentals. I was hopeless. I was lapped five times. I swore never to go to a bike race again.' But times and attitudes changed, and (on a different bike, again paid for from his paper round) he entered another race several months later and won. It wasn't long — 1952 and 1953 — before he became Belgian amateur champion in Brussels and Deerlijk. He turned pro immediately afterwards.

When he started, Rik van Steenbergen was on the stage. When van Looy, another *Antwerpenaar*, turned up, the press named him first Rik II and then The

Emperor. van Looy didn't complain. Nor could van Steenbergen, since van Looy won the first pro race he entered, at Kortenaken. And, for that matter, he won again the next afternoon in Heist-op-den-Berg.

Then came two Tours of Flanders, Liège–Bastogne–Liège, three Paris–Roubaix, two Paris–Tours, Milan–San Remo, the Tour of Lombardy, three Ghent–Wevelgems and the Flemish Arrow.

'I had to fight to dominate van Steenbergen,' he said. 'When you're at the top, you fight to stay there. You don't give that away easily. I was the same when Eddy Merckx was coming up. It is for the newcomer to prove himself.'

Some people could be fended off. Merckx could not. By that time van Looy all but controlled Belgian racing and he didn't take well to the matinée idol from Brussels stealing his ground. van Looy is not the kind of man to take a rival into his heart; he didn't with van Steenbergen and I doubt he ever did with Merckx. There are many who crossed van Looy or foiled him and who lived to regret their impudence.

But Merckx, in the end, triumphed.

'To beat him, I would have had to have been born several years later. He impressed me from the start. On a good day, maybe one in ten, I could beat him. For me, he is the greatest rider of all time.'

And it was age, and maybe Merckx as well, that forced van Looy out.

'Everything I did,' he recalls, 'I did impulsively. If I thought I could win, I'd win. If I couldn't, I wanted one of my team to win. I stopped racing on instinct. I just stopped. I told my wife as we were driving and I don't think she believed me, but it was true, and I don't regret it.'

There were no Sinatra-like or even Anquetil-like farewell performances. In his last race, van Looy missed the break but still won the bunch sprint to come eighth. Those who were there, just like those who saw Eddy Merckx in the Omloop van het Waasland some years later, didn't realise they'd seen a bit of history fade to black.

Both men rode for the last time in insignificant races; neither realised at the start that they were lining up for the last time.

'By that time, I wasn't as impulsive as I used to be. I'd learned to spread myself out a bit more, as you do when you get older. To keep your strength better. I was 37 when I stopped. I wasn't worn out. On the right days, I still felt like a star and I'd ride like one. I could still have won a classic if I'd really wanted to. But off the bike, it was different. It was harder and harder to go out training every day.

'I didn't want to lumber on, like an old man. So that was it. I stopped. Curtains.'

Much more than van Steenbergen, and in quite a different manner from Merckx, van Looy controlled Belgian racing. He brought in sponsors and organised teams. He was friends with the agents and the criterium organisers, who were far more important then than now. He had fingers in many different operations and his influence was considerable.

Benoni Beheyt was a good rider until the day at Ronsse when he beat van Looy for the world championship in 1963. Neither would speak of the incident for years except in the most diplomatic words.

'Beheyt had agreed to ride for me,' van Looy says now, as he has said for years, 'but you can't blame a rider who sees an opportunity like that so close to hand and then reaches out and takes it.'

Unfortunately, Beheyt did more than reach out. The official explanation was that he'd stretched out his arm to avoid a collision, that he'd only been fending van Looy back to safety. Years afterwards he admitted that, Maradonna-style, he had reached out and then gone further — as far as tugging the Emperor's jersey.

'It's still a painful memory and a great disappointment,' says van Looy. 'I was convinced I was going to win. There were seven Belgians in the front group in the last lap and everyone had agreed to ride for me. For me, the whole world turned upside down when Beheyt made out he had cramp and then attacked me. But looking back, I can understand his reaction.'

For all the oil slicks of diplomacy, Beheyt was never allowed to be a happy man again.

'I believe in having a top man in a team,' says van Looy, to whom it rarely occurred that that top man wouldn't be him. 'Coppi taught me that. I was impressed by the way he got himself ready for each season. I got to know about that when I was riding for Touvring in 1954. It really appealed to me.

'I was born a leader. It's my nature, but I couldn't just walk in and say "I'm going to lead the Red Guard" [the nickname for van Looy's successive teams]. It took me two years to prove that I could do it.'

Briek Schotte was his first real team leader. Jos Schils, the Belgian champion, was next on the ladder, then Germain Derycke, who'd won Paris–Roubaix, and then Willy Vannitsen. van Looy, if he was anything at all, was fifth.

But by the time he got his own team, Faema, there was no doubting who was the boss. And there was no shortage of riders to choose. While Britain had Brian Robinson and English was a rare language in the bunch, tiny Belgium — no larger than East Anglia — had 279 professionals in 1956, half as many again as neighbouring France and five times as many as Italy. One in seven Belgians holding a racing licence was riding either as a professional or an independent, a semi-professional.

'The first time I'd been able to pick any team-mates was when I was with Schotte, when after a while Lomme Driessens [most recently the guiding light behind Freddy Maertens and now an old man in Brussels] said I could choose a couple.

'But when I got to Faema, I chose them all, on the basis of their qualities and what they'd achieved. In the classics, everyone had to ride for me; in the other races, they were able to ride for whoever was in the best position on the road. It was that richness which produced so many successes among my team-mates.'

van Looy makes his teams sound like an amicable co-operative, a happy collective working for an amiable boss who regularly threw sovereigns of gratitude into their midst. Talk to Vin Denson, though, and you get a different story. Denson rode for van Looy when the two were sponsored by a margarine company called Solo.

'It was Solo by name and solo by nature,' Denson recalls. 'You rode for van Looy and did whatever he wanted, including the fetching of beers, which he had a great fondness for in mid-race. *Domestiques* were reduced to chasing long miles to bring the great man a bottle of Stella.'

When van Looy climbed off or had a bad day, team-mates didn't so much ride for whoever was best placed as fight against each other to no great general benefit. That van Looy could stamp discipline and fear across a bunch of ill-educated, table-sprawling, uncouth Belgians with no team sense of their own shows the strength of personality that the Emperor could display.

Indeed a born leader.

He confesses to never having started a tour with the ambition of winning it. He did win, of course, but he insists it was more by piling up stages, like building bricks, until they became so substantial that nobody could knock them over. He even insists that had his employers allowed him to ride the Tour de France then, in the days before Anquetil at least, he might have won. But the Tour then was for national teams, and van Looy had an Italian sponsor; the Italians told him to ride the Giro instead. van Looy regrets it to this day.

In 1963, released to ride, he came tenth. On the stage from Pau to Bagnères-de-Bigorre, across the Tourmalet and the Aubisque, he lost 10 minutes. It was the same margin that Anquetil had on him by the finish in Paris.

Even so, tales are rife that he rode as much with money in mind as eventual success. Cynics say that there were still criteriums during the Tour in those days and that van Looy could push up his price with a Tour win or two, then return to Belgium for more start money than he could hope to win in the Tour and win prizes against a field diminished precisely because the best had gone to the Tour de France. van Looy, doubtless, would see it otherwise.

And when he had nothing more to ride, he was at a loose end. He kept horses, helped out with the IJsboerke team, and then he took to driving about with reporters from *Sport 70*, adding his comments to the day's racing.

But there was still a void.

The Flemish *wielerschool*, where riders are coached, weighed, guided and taken on trips to Spain, is where his heart lies now. It was closed when I arrived and the venetian blinds were drawn. van Looy, who was collecting papers before going to see his doctor about a back pain, couldn't stay long. (The doctor, Dr Claes, is the one van Looy used throughout his career and works now at the bike school.)

The school is part of a huge sports ground. Its politics are immensely complicated, as befits a small country with three official languages. There are more than a hundred riders there all winter, some staying a week, some just coming for Monday-to-Friday training. The youngest is 12, the oldest 25. A few are professionals. van Hooydonck is among those who learned their skills there. van Looy sees them come and go.

If he could wave his wand now, he'd have the toppers ride in different teams. At the moment Belgium maintains a permanent amateur team and they ride as such in all the big amateur races.

'But if I had my way, they wouldn't,' he says. 'I'd have them riding against each other. It's the only way to improve. They need to fight more. I refuse to believe there's no more talent in Flanders. But that's why there's no new van Steenbergen, van Looy or Merckx.

'They take the easy way out.'

But then, once again, you're up against politics, and van Looy's influence is no longer what it was.

7 JACQUES ANQUETIL (1934–1987)

Beyond the cinemas and dossers of Leicester Square there stood a French restaurant, not large but well thought of. In the Easter of 1964, Alan Gayfer, the editor of *Cycling*, rang to book a table.

'For lunch at 11.45?' he suggested.

'Is not possible,' said the French owner. 'Not open so early. Nobody want lunch that early.'

'But I know how good your food is and I can't come later because I have two guests and we have to be at Herne Hill in the afternoon.'

'Is not possible. Sorry.' He moved to put the phone back on its cradle.

'Then Monsieur Anquetil will have to go elsewhere,' said Gayfer. The telephone line from Leicester Square to *Cycling*'s offices above the Golden Egg in Fleet Street carried the sound of a small French explosion.

'*Mon dieu!* Jacques Anquetil? You are very welcome, m'sieur. Your table will be ready.' The man who feared Rik van Looy was clearly respected by others.

Two things stand out. The first is that the restaurateur gave Gayfer the bill but refused payment — 'You and your guests are *my* guests,' he said — and that Anquetil, having seen the bill but not heard the generosity, offered Gayfer his share. When Gayfer told him he had had a free meal simply for being Anquetil, the Tour winner guffawed in astonishment.

'In France,' he roared, 'they try to charge me double!'

'You forget,' Gayfer reflected in 1993, the year he died, 'that a man we take to be a hero was seen in France as a target to be fleeced.'

The other point is that Gayfer interested Anquetil, the world's greatest time-triallist, in riding a '25' on the Southend Road, then the best course in Britain.

'He was intrigued,' said Gayfer, 'and he was keen to ride if he could get £1,000 — in 1964, remember. He was asking what hills there would be, and Tom Simpson, who was with us, assured him that the average British time-trial never rose more than 200 feet the whole way.

'And he said "Well, that's no problem, then."

'I asked him what time he thought he would do for 25 miles. Bear in mind that he had no idea what the RTTC best was. He said 46 minutes. The record was 54-23, to Bas Breedon. With no guidance, he had estimated eight minutes off the competition record.'

It never happened, even though a timber merchant called Vic Jenner was keen to put up the money. Jenner died shortly afterwards, and so, early in life, did Anquetil. In his last years the Frenchman looked ghostly, the result many said of the drugs he campaigned for. But Anquetil died of cancer, in his home town of Rouen on November 18, 1987.

Jacques Anquetil rarely came to Britain. He rode the wind-cracked acres of Herne Hill and he came as a television commentator to the world championships and to a fascinatingly dull stage of the Tour de France near Plymouth.

Barrel-chested, shark-eyed with high cheekbones and coiffured blond hair, he was a star against the clock when post-war time-trialling was at its peak in Britain. He infuriated the opposition, and sometimes France, by winning against the clock what the more valiant gained in the mountains.

Another veteran journalist, Jock Wadley, once played bridge late into the night at his mansion near the Seine. Next morning Anquetil rode a race. It was that contradiction — the cavalier attitude, the cold calculation — that made Anquetil an enigma. Here was a man who spoke for French cycling but also for the right to take drugs, and that at a time when colleagues were dropping dead or going crackers on the stuff.

In 1967, the man with whom Gayfer and Anquetil had lunched in Leicester Square died on the climb of Mont Ventoux. Whatever else might have killed Tom Simpson, drugs played a part. Anquetil spoke regularly for the right to take drugs, equating them with the aspirin a schoolteacher took to cure a headache before a maths lesson. Anquetil led a walking strike against drug tests in the Tour de France of 1966, in Bordeaux. He was quietly dropped from France's team for the world championship and the Tour de France.

Newspapers once reported how a doctor followed him to the showers, insisting on his test.

'You're too late,' Anquetil said angrily, pointing at the soapy water running down the hole. 'It's all gone down there. I can't oblige you with any more for a while. I'm not a fountain.'

Anquetil wrote in *France Dimanche* in 1967: 'Yes, I dope myself.' He wrote of how, as he weakened, he reached into his shorts for a pill which would give him 'the invigorating crack of the whip.' He added: 'You would be a fool to imagine that a professional cyclist who rides 235 days a year in all temperatures and conditions can hold up without a stimulant.'

Later the same year, he was fined £84 and banned for two years by a court in Antwerp, Belgium, after being found positive at the track on the city outskirts. It took until February 1969 to overturn the decision on the grounds that there had been no second urine sample for a check test.

He wasn't alone. Roger Rivière, who held the world hour record in 1957 and 1958 and whose career ended when he rode over the side of the col du Perjuret in 1960, also admitted in *France Dimanche* that he'd taken drugs. Specifically, he had used them for the hour record, which he considered unbeatable without dope. In a court in St Etienne in France, Rivière later confessed he had become a drug addict and had taken more than 32,000 tablets in three years. He was fined for illegal drug use.

He was at the trackside to watch Anquetil beat him with 47.5km (29.5 miles) on 52 ˇ 13, a gear of 108 inches. But then Anquetil's manager, Raphaël Géminiani, urged the doctor to test his rider at the Canoica-Lembro hotel and not, as the doctor insisted, at the track. There was a scuffle and Anquetil felt obliged to intervene.

Dr Giuliano Marena stayed at the edge of the Vigorelli in Rome for hours before leaving for home in Florence. Officialdom denied Anquetil the record (which was beaten a few weeks later by the Belgian, Ferdi Bracke, anyway).

Anquetil said afterwards: 'I didn't and don't intend to escape the test, but it must take place under circumstances far different from those at the velodrome. These "gentlemen" of the UCI want revenge on me for something. They were hounding me, and they caught me — and they had been waiting for this opportunity for a long time.'

In fact a French federation doctor took a sample when Anquetil got back to Rouen, pointing out that a test was valid up to 48 hours after the race. But for the UCI, the issue was closed.

Anquetil saw himself as a shop steward, or a diplomat. Many supported him, even though the years make his views naive and even sinister. Anquetil was a dignified, gentlemanly man, proud of his craft. That point should not be forgotten. He brought cyclists from the semi-serfdom of the 1950s just as Greg LeMond brought the sport into another commercial reality 20 years later. If, as he reasoned, no other professional would be humiliated by peeing into a bottle behind a canvas screen, at the height of his triumph and while eight thousand spectators (Anquetil took 60 per cent of the gate money) cheered or even jeered, then why should a racing cyclist? Why, even more, should the best racing cyclist in the world?

Jacques Anquetil was an agricultural student at the Collège Technique de Sotteville, near his home in Quincampoix, when he joined the Association Cycliste Sotteville, in the suburbs of Rouen. The area is unremarkable, the town industrial, notable largely for being where Joan of Arc was burned in the market square in 1431. He came under the wing of a cycle-shop owner called André Boucher, who paced him with his Derny motorcycle and encouraged his egg-shaped crouch and toes-down pedalling — a technique which Barry Hoban deliberately copied.

It took little time to make a mark. He won the amateur road championship in Carcassonne and the Grand Prix de France time-trial, beating the favourite by 12 minutes in 50 miles. He rode the last 76 miles of Paris–Normandy at better than 26mph, leaving the runner-up nine minutes down and the fourth man a good quarter of an hour back.

He was 19. Unknown to him, a parcel of press cuttings was sent from Normandy to the La Perle bicycle company. It was sent by the firm's representative in Normandy to its team manager, Francis Pélissier. The old Tour star read them with interest. This young Anquetil, he thought, could be just the *gamin* he wanted with whom to counter the all-dominant but adult Louison Bobet.

A month later, Anquetil was a minute up in the Grand Prix des Nations at 20km and rode the entire 88 miles at 24.8mph. Afterwards he said: 'It was no better than the end of Paris–Normandy.' Pélissier, waggled the cigarette between his lips and said drily: 'You ain't seen nothing yet.' He signed Anquetil for La Perle.

The boy was unstoppable. He took Fausto Coppi's hour record at his second attempt and, still only 23, travelled to Nantes for the start of his first Tour de France.

Now in those days the Tour was *disputé* by national teams, a response to accusations that the race had become over-commercial. It made it more interesting, backing France or Belgium or even, occasionally, Britain. But commercially it was a problem, since riders who were rivals all year found national neighbourliness difficult for the three weeks of the Tour. Strange combines formed. The Tour meant as much to the stars as it did for hangers-on, for whom helping in a star's difficult moment assured a contract for the coming year. It didn't much matter if that star was, for the three weeks, in a different team.

Anquetil's *agitprop* started early. He would not, he said, ride as number two to Bobet.

'I would rather ride in a regional team than with him,' he said. Much huffing and puffing and bad blood followed before Bobet told Europe 1, the radio station: 'I've decided not to ride the Tour. I'm not psyched up to ride two big tours. I want to live like everybody else, to swim in the sea and to spend time with my children. I've done enough to earn a rest.'

Bobet's supporters also pulled out and Anquetil was left *chef d'équipe* of Young France. It wasn't the last time that politics and conniving would push him ahead. Nor was there satisfaction for Bobet, who was in the crowd in Charleroi in Belgium when Anquetil took the yellow jersey. He still had it at the end.

Anquetil, unfortunately, suffered from what subsequently became known as Maertens syndrome. Freddy Maertens was a rubbery-faced Belgian who, for three years, could win more than 50 races a season because of his sprint. But the more he won, the more he was disliked, because the world loves a man who can win alone, best of all in the mountains, and not someone who relies on a calculated gift.

Anquetil was no sprinter. He was, as one team manager put it, 'the man who can drop nobody but whom nobody can drop.' And, since time-trialling is a precise business with no hidden cards, Anquetil could and did predict his victories. Cassius Clay was loved for it; Anquetil became hated.

He won in 1957 and 1961 and only a change in the rules and the arrival of a big bumbling farmworker from the peasant south saved him. In 1962, the Tour de France switched to trade teams for the first time since 1930. The French could therefore ride legitimately against each other and the country could support the villain it chose. It was a shame, Jacques Goddet said, to leave the old order, but it didn't work

Raymond Poulidor rode for Mercier, one of France's oldest teams and one of the few still backed in the main by a bike company. That, and his slow-talking country honesty, appealed to rural France, which dismissed as poisonous babble accusations that their man had *les jambes du cheval, la tête d'une vache* — the legs of a horse, the brain of a cow. Poulidor's nick-name, *pou-pou*, is either an affectionate diminutive or a contraction of doll-brain, according to the side you take. He disliked it, anyway.

Anquetil was a travelling circus, taking his team from the aperitif company St Raphaël to Ford and eventually to the Bic ballpoint factory. He was the city slicker to Poulidor's ditch-digger. For year after year they came head to head, irritated at times by the eccentric Spaniard Federico Bahamontes, a brilliant climber who ate ice cream at the top of cols rather than descend them alone.

One of the sport's most famous pictures shows Anquetil, Poulidor and Bahamontes hub to hub in the Alps. But Poulidor never won. He never even wore the yellow jersey. He came second in 1964, 1965 and 1974, third in 1962, 1966, 1969 and 1972. Largely it was Anquetil's fault and the country turned against him. It wanted a human, not a robot. Delight — 'An-que-til, An-que-til,' France chanted — turned to hissing.

And then, in the spring of 1965, Raphaël Géminiani had an idea. In 1957, Géminiani had been a team-mate at Anquetil's first Tour; now he was his manager. And desperate to raise his charge's standing, and possibly to keep his own job with St Raphaël, he pointed out a possible double.

'You are the Zatopek of cycling,' he said, referring to the Czech who had won the Olympic marathon at his first attempt after winning the 5,000 and 10,000 metres as well. 'Ride the Dauphiné–Libéré as a prelude to Bordeaux–Paris and I'll bet half a million francs on your chances.'

It was, if nothing else, a grand gamble. The Dauphiné–Libéré was a mountainous, week-long stage race, one of the best in France. Bordeaux–Paris is the longest race in the world, 345 miles that year, much of it flat-out behind motorcycle pacers. The Dauphiné finished at Avignon at 5pm on May 29, the second began at midnight the same day in Bordeaux. A check on the map will show you how far the two are from each other.

The papers called it the maddest, most dangerous publicity stunt they had heard. Some demanded it was called off. But Géminiani reasoned that a rider leaving a stage race might be tired, but his body is fit, his system used to demands. Bordeaux–Paris should be considered simply the final stage of the Dauphiné–Libéré.

But things did not go that simply. For a start, the Dauphiné proved a battle with Poulidor. And second, the last stage was through freezing fog. Anquetil, Poulidor and a young professional called Lucien Aimar finished the last *en ligne* stage together, shivering, their eyebrows knotted with ice.

'I've never known anything like it,' Anquetil shivered. 'If I hadn't been the *maillot jaune*, I would have quit.' He rode the final time-trial, won by 13 seconds, and at 5pm climbed the rostrum, received his acclaim like a gentleman but just a mite hurried, and then ran to Géminiani's Ford Taunus.

The timetable then was breathless. Pursued by journalists, Anquetil reached the Hôtel Crillon at 5.20, showered, had a massage, and then had steak, cheese, strawberry tart and two beers. By 5.55 he was back on the road at 90mph, tyres squealing, police motorcyclists clearing his way.

There were 40 miles to the airport at Nîmes-Garons and they got there at 6.30.

'I'm shattered from that car rally of a journey,' Anquetil told the crowds as his masseur worked on him on an airport couch. 'What a story.' Reporters and television crews followed him to the aircraft. By 6.50 the door was shut and the small business jet began rolling towards Bordeaux. Not until his hotel on the banks of the Gironde did he manage just an hour's sleep.

Bordeaux–Paris starts at midnight. It is a long way, and the hundred miles until dawn are at racing pace but restrained, in tracksuits and woollen hats. At Châtellerault the weary group collects the portly pacers, their stomachs preposterously straining their racing jerseys, their fat legs pushed outwards for shelter as they pedal antique *moto-bicyclettes* towards Paris.

Not for a moment did Anquetil think he could get that far. His face was lined, his eyes bleary. He complained of pain in his thighs. He protested after 50 miles that he couldn't get his breath.

To make matters worse, an ambitious Frenchman called Claude Valdois had ignored the agreement to stop before Châtellerault and disrobe. Instead, he had discarded his tracksuit at the back of the field, in the darkness, and attacked the moment the others halted.

Anquetil was furious and shouted at Vin Denson, a Briton in the race, to get off up the road after him.

'I jumped after him with my shorts half on, fastening my braces, and Stablinski, the other Ford man riding for Anquetil, followed with one sock on and still trying to get his heels in his shoes,' Denson recalled.

This gave rise to one of the bizarrest stories of the race, because Denson caught Valdois just before Châtellerault and won a prize for collecting his Derny first. He and his pacemaker then headed off in a rosy glow towards Paris. Unfortunately, Anquetil's demands meant Denson hadn't answered nature's demands and, when they had a five-minute lead, he ran to a tree for a relief.

Normally five minutes would have been enough, but Denson was the star of the moment, surrounded by cameras and crowds of Frenchmen urging him on. And he caught stage-fright. As he stood behind his tree, quaking with embarrassment and distress, Anquetil, the man he was supposed to be protecting, swept by in a snarl of motorcycle exhaust.

The hammers were falling on Anquetil by the minute. Valdois was caught but now François Mahé had a six-minute lead and one by one the others cleared off after him ... Melckembeck ... Valdois ... Pamard ... Le Menn.

But the day as well as the race was warming up. The headwind had subdued, and at Chartres Anquetil responded successfully when Stablinski attacked. For hour after hour they rode like bees, swarming, dispersing, stinging and generally making life hell.

Tom Simpson was there, and Stablinski, and Anquetil, hundreds of miles in their legs, their eyes reddened by the night, the exhaustion and the lack of sleep.

But Anquetil, who had slept less than any of them after the freezing mountains of the Dauphiné–Libéré, was an automaton.

He came into St-Rémy-les-Chevreuse ahead of the group, accelerated on the climb through Buc and opened a gap on the straight roads into Paris. The white and pale blue jersey, crouched and sweat-stained, made its way through the minor paths into the Parc des Princes, roads that Anquetil knew well because the Tour in those days finished with a time-trial into the big old track. And there, turning right on the shallow bankings, he finished Bordeaux–Paris.

Several minutes later, Stablinski and Simpson followed him in.

'Tough?', someone asked him.

'More than that,' he said drily, and he left for his first real sleep in 48 hours and 400 miles.

Five Tours de France fell to Jacques Anquetil, as many as Fausto Coppi before him and as many as Eddy Merckx and Bernard Hinault afterwards. There were no world championships, few national championships, few classics. Anquetil, the man whom nobody could drop, was a stage-race specialist who calculated his victory by the length of the time-trial stages. He rode his last race, on the track in Antwerp, on December 27, 1969, and never rode a bike again. He spent his retirement running his farm — he was the son of a strawberry grower — directing his bicycle and quarry companies and commentating for television. To the last, he was bitter that the French sports minister had sent a telegram to congratulate Ferdi Bracke, a Belgian, on beating Anquetil's record — but had never sent Anquetil a telegram for beating Rivière's.

He became the race director of Paris–Nice, which he won five times, a record which fell to Sean Kelly in 1987. Anquetil helped him celebrate.

Here was a man who spoke for drugs but, when he developed cancer in 1986, declined surgery and went on working, ghost-like, as a commentator at the Tour de France. Doctors operated on his stomach after the Tour, but on the morning of November 18, 1987, in the St-Hilaire clinic near Rouen, he died aged 53. It hit the French press in the way De Gaulle's death had struck.

The following year the Tour passed his black marble grave at Quincampoix as it travelled from Rouen to the start at Neufchâtel-en-Bray. The riders stopped to pay homage, and each year on the weekend after Ascension Day hundreds of cyclo-touristes ride in his homage between Quincampoix and Genneville. In 1983 the 2,000 residents of Quincampoix named their sports centre after their greatest son. But France in general is confused to this day whether it was celebrating a wise or a foolish hero.

8 GRAHAM WEBB (1944–)

The neighbours call him Mr Vepp. He's still lugubrious and unreasonably tall, but a beard now gives him a Messianic appearance. He's the world champion who never came home, the man who never fitted the team. Britain has never won a men's road championship since him. Yet he's overlooked now as much as he was at the time.

In 1967, Mr Vepp unfolded himself across his bike and raced so fast along a stretch of Dutch motorway that no one could survive alongside him. It should have been a beginning. Instead, it was the beginning of the end.

To find Graham Webb, you have to ride west from Herentals, back past Antwerp, and on into the centre of Ghent. Then you turn right along the dismal industrial road that shadows the river. You go for eight miles like that, hoping something around you will lift the heart. And then, just as you think it never will, you come back into the countryside. And then you reach Graham Webb's village. He lives in a modern house, in a road called Canary Lane in Dutch, with an MG-B parked outside. He forgets the odd word of English after all these years but he's still very British.

His enemies told me he was 'a big thick bugger', but that's neither fair nor true. Yet time after time there were incidents in his life which, if you weren't to interpret them as simple naive heroism, you might mistake for outright dumbo-ism.

As a kid, he kept riding from Birmingham to Gloucester and back until he could do it without falling into a ditch — literally, falling into a ditch with exhaustion. No other reason. He did it just to see if he could do it. And when he couldn't, he carried on doing it until he could.

'I just enjoyed it. I enjoyed suffering, I suppose. I still do,' he said through the beard on that long mournful face. Even the tale of his first race has a melancholy humour. He started not knowing what to do and finished not realising he'd won.

'I met someone in a racing club, the Solihull. So I went to this club — I was 16 — and there were a hundred blokes milling about in this hall and I just stood there watching them. Nobody knew me and I didn't know them. This went on for a few weeks, but no one spoke to me and I was very shy.

'Mick Shakespeare came up one night and he said "Are you riding the club 25?" I said "What's that?" He told me and I said "Yeah, all right, what do I have to do?"

'I'd got a tee-shirt and a pair of cut-off jeans and some tennis pumps. I was watching them get into this racing gear, and eventually I got fed up with all these blokes changing and I thought "When's this race going to start?" It should have started at six o'clock and these blokes were still getting changed. I didn't know it was every minute a bloke off.

'So I thought bugger this and I rode up to the start. The timekeeper said "You're too late, you'll have to wait."

'Well, they pushed me off and I was 10 minutes late starting and I thought I had to catch all the blokes in front of me to win the race. I changed into top gear straight away on this old Hercules Harlequin and I knocked my pump off the down tube and I had to wait for the cars to come past, then turn round and pick my pump up.

'I quickly caught someone and I waited for him. And he was telling me "clear off, clear off" — very unsociable, I thought. I rode on, went round the turn in the road, came back, and the chain jumped off between the block and the frame. So I had to get off the bike, and I'd got a whole tool kit with me, spanner, oil can, cloth for cleaning my hands and so on, and this was wrapped round my seat tube with a spare inner tube. I had to undo the back wheel, put the chain on, do up the wheel nuts, put everything behind the seat tube and carry on.

'Well, I got to the finish and I looked around ... "'ell, what happens now?" So I cleared off and went home.

'Anyway, Thursday night, back to the clubhouse and the same thing, just sitting in the corner looking at all these people, and one of these chaps, Graham Kelly, he came over and said "Is your name Graham Webb?"

'He said ... "That time-trial on Sunday, you had the fastest time." I went as red as a beetroot. I'd done 1-1-31 and if I'd started on time and not had any trouble, I'd have broken the hour on this old bike, maybe. So in the Solihull I was famous from that day on and everybody wanted to talk to me.'

Frankly, I've never met a man more miserable about his amateur career in Britain than Graham Webb. It doesn't surprise me at all that he's stayed in Belgium. Nor that the BCF has never used him as a coach or a manager, although it does astonish him.

I'll fill you in later on some of those grouses, but the next important bit of the story is that in 1966 he was so cheesed off that he and his wife sold everything and moved to Hilversum, east of Amsterdam. His mentor was Charles Ruys, the old Dutch sailor who swore like a bosun's parrot.

Webb's first race was in Breda near Wim van Est. It was what the Dutch call *rotweer* — snow, hail, wind, the lot.

'It was running up cobbled roads, and they were using a dirt track on the side of the road with holes you could put a whole wheel in, and they were covered with water.

'It was really thrilling because I had something I could dig my teeth into. I was pushing and shoving all the time, and I'd get to the back of the echelon, riding on the grass, on the road, on the cobbles, on the road — up the dykes and down them, and I was really enjoying myself.

'And there was this one chap and he was really dangerous, and he kept pushing me, and I got to the back of the echelon and he was trying not to come to the front. And he was shouting "*Pas op, pas op!*" ["watch it, mate"] all the time. I don't know if it was very sporting of me or not, but I put him in the ditch, not really to get rid of him, but I wanted the other riders to know I wasn't going to play around. It was only a grass ditch and I knew he wasn't going to hurt himself, and after that I didn't have to push any more.

'At one stage we went up this dyke. The blokes in front started to slip on the wet cobbles and mud, and I was having to take the corners wider and wider, and I slipped into the grass and over the dyke and into the sea — seven metres. I was covered in black mud. I dragged my bike out of the water and up the bank, and I got back on and started chasing. I caught a few who'd got shot off and finished 16th, covered in slime and freezing cold, in my first race.

'Anyway, I was more or less famous from my first race in Holland. I was a hero, and I didn't know why. A hero for being 16th. I couldn't understand it.'

The next race was a criterium on a kilometre course with seven corners a lap, on *klinkers* (a bumpy surface of stone tiles set like a parquet floor). The sprinters went for the primes. Webb didn't understand and went with them. Shades of the Solihull '25'.

'We came round for the first prime and I took it and I was piling the pressure on in the corners and I was left with one chap on my wheel. There were no real long stretches to burn him off, so I thought I'd have to get rid of him. I went into the chicane. I thought if he tries to follow me he'll crash into a wall. I had this feeling I could corner better than anyone.

'Sure enough, he wrapped himself round a lamp-post trying to follow me, which was very courageous of him, trying to the death to follow me. I've got a lot of respect for that. Anyway I was away. I could have lapped them but I wasn't sure whether I'd have to sprint again for the primes. So I just left them hanging there.

'I won 98 primes plus the *klassement* [the prime points competition]. I'd won enough money to pay for six months' bed and board. So I knew then that I didn't have to work.'

Now, personally, I'm not accustomed to winning races. I'm certainly not accustomed to lapping one, let alone lapping one three times. Webb did that several times. There's no way I can properly describe to you what that means — to lap a Dutch criterium three times.

I tried to put the question with sensitivity.

'When you rode through the bunch for the third time,' I said, 'what did you detect?'

It produced a slow smile.

'Well, I wouldn't lap them round the back of the circuit. I would wait until the finish area, where the most people were, because I wanted to make a name for myself. And usually the riders were all huddled to one side of the road and I'd take the other side of the road and wait for the crowd and I'd just ride past them.

'And they'd start jumping to get on my wheel and they just couldn't. I could go 6kmh faster than anyone else.'

Ah, they said, you'll turn pro next year, inwardly rejoicing that they'd be let off the hook.

But nobody made an offer. Nobody. I've never met anyone in Holland who suggested he was an awkward cuss — although you'll find one or two in Britain who remember him that way — but it does nevertheless follow the pattern that Mr Vepp never fitted easily into a team, or the team around him.

When he was 19, he entered the Archer GP, an early-season event of some standing near Gerrards Cross in Buckinghamshire. They put him in the overflow race, which depressed him even though he won it 'dead easy.'

A place in the world's team time-trial led nowhere and he threw himself into time-trialling — something from which, he says with biblical zeal, all young riders should be protected.

'I went for the "25" record, which I didn't realise then didn't mean a thing. I rode a time-trial every weekend up to the Brentwood and did the second ride in under 55 minutes, on an atrocious day. And then the year after that I virtually stopped racing. It was just boring. I wasn't interested.'

In '66 he broke the British hour record that Les West had held.

'Even though I was going really well, it was still Hugh Porter and Harry Jackson in the pursuit, and if they did the worst ride in Britain they'd still have gone. They could tell the best jokes, I suppose. It's still the same now, isn't it?

'The thing that really knocked me back was that I was shortlisted for the Olympics in Tokyo and the last trials for the team pursuit were in Welwyn. I'd gone down with Tommy Godwin and we started with Dave Whitfield and Brendan McKeown and Harry Jackson or Trevor Bull, I can't remember.

'I punctured twice before I'd actually clocked a time. I'd only got two pairs of wheels to my name, track wheels, so we had to start the team again, but I couldn't get a wheel off anyone. No one would lend me a wheel, so I didn't make the Olympics. It was as simple as that.

'I felt terribly bitter about it. Terribly.

'I can understand if it was true that I didn't get picked because I didn't fit in the team. It may have been my own fault. I see it now in my youngest daughter. She's that way too. She's got tremendous talent but she does the opposite because she doesn't want to stand out.

'The thing in the British track team then was to demoralise the rest as much as possible, and if you succeeded at that, you'd succeeded completely in the British track team's eyes. Fred Booker was all right, and Trevor Bull. But it was sort of trying to defeat one another, and that was destroying the whole team every year.

'And the only objective was to get picked and go for the trip, and once you'd been picked, that was the end of it. I never heard anyone say "I want to be world champion or Olympic champion or do well." That was very depressing.'

Which is why he went to Holland.

'I thought they were the best riders, the best races in the world, and I felt I could learn something in Holland.

'The last road race before I left England was somewhere near Portsmouth. We started the race, and after a mile we went up this steep hill and the two blokes in front were gasping and they called me to go through. So I went to the front, and at the top of the hill I went to move over and let them through, and there was no one in sight. So I thought I'd carry on a bit, and I just rode to the finish by myself. I didn't even have to extend myself.

'I said I'd wait and see who was second before I went for a wash, and I had to wait 13 minutes before the second man came over the line.'

He rode the world championships on the Amsterdam track in 1967 and had a barney with the team manager, Dave Handley. Charles Ruys didn't show up, and Webb fell in instead with 'Fat Albert' — Albert Buerick, the anglophile Belgian who had been friend to Tom Simpson, who'd died earlier that same year.

Beurick took him to Destelbergen in Belgium, found him a race, and Webb lapped the field twice on a four-kilometre loop.

'I took another Englishman round with me — Geoff Wiles, I think, but I'm not sure. Anyway I took him round with me and I won that race, and it was my first road race in Belgium. It was a lot easier than in Holland.'

In the second race he got a good lead, but the surface was dangerous and he'd had enough. Partway round he nipped off, hid behind a car, and went off to have a shower while the chasers blew their own heads off.

Next day he rode 300km to the German border to meet the road team.

'There was a completely different attitude. Friendly, jolly, completely different. The attitude it should have been, not at all like the track team.

'I started like a kilometre time-trial, just as fast, just as hard, and I had to ride flat out two or three miles to get to the front.

'And I stayed at the front, did my turn, and after a while it started getting easier. After 50km it was the first time I looked round, and we were away, with 13 of us. All the best blokes were at the front, except De Vlaeminck, who got up later.

'And we went up the climb, which is something no one ever knows about — if you write this it'll be the first time it's ever been known — we went up the climb, and I looked back and I could see a bunch with an English jersey.

'And I dropped off the break and back to the second bunch and it was Pete Buckley, and I towed him up to the break. I said "Come on, I could do with your help."

'But during that time, four blokes had got away from that break — Ampler, Monseré, Conti and Benn — but I hadn't seen them go and I didn't know they were away. I got back up and started working again and I was looking for Buckley and he'd got shot off again. He'd just got shot off again and I couldn't understand why. It was just the level of racing I was used to compared to the English blokes.

'And then I discovered there were these four blokes ahead, so no one would work any more. There was an Italian in the four-man break and three Italians with me, there was a Belgian away and I had De Vlaeminck, and Pijnen wasn't going to work, so I said we're racing for fifth place here, and in a world championship there's not even a medal.

'So the last lap I went to the front, with the wind coming from the left, and I stayed to the right. I could have got up on my own, but I thought when I get there I'm going to be knackered. I'm going to be fifth anyway. I started to work out how I was going to do it. I would open the sprint slowly. The best blokes would stay with me. I went to the front, and I reckoned if we could get them in sight before the last climb, someone's going to try to jump over to the leaders. And come to the last, sure enough we got them in sight, and they were attacking as well, and the speed was going up and down, and they started coming from behind me, trying to jump up to them, which is what I wanted.

'So we went up the last climb and they were attacking all the time and I stayed on the back, just leaving them to it, just being towed up, which was perfect.

It lasted only a day, but Simpson wore yellow in the Tour de France. There are still few enough British *maillots jaunes* to fit into a single telephone box.

Ghent–Wevelgem 1963. Two Belgians, Michel van Aerde and Benoni Beheyt, fight it out by the kerb, while Tom Simpson is theatrical on the right. But why is Simpson's hand already on the brakes?

Simpson's finest hour — world champion 1967. He was later ticked off for wearing his Peugeot rather than his GB jersey to the podium. The chubby man in the Maes Pils jacket to the left is famous in all Simpson's world championship pictures for the odd expressions he pulls. He stands on the line as Simpson wins, and here he's the only person in the crowd with his back to the new champion.

I had the idea once of offering Peter Post 10 shillings to wear a Westerley Road Club racing hat. He was a legend in six-day racing. Others have won more races since, but none has been such a hard case. Rivals called him a bastard; his wife calls him 'Treasure'.

Cigar smoke, noise, the rumble of wheels and the smell of chip fat in the dark. They were life winter after winter for Peter Post, the hard man of the six-day. His partner here is Fritz Pfenninger of Switzerland.

Left:

Brian Robinson. It's 1961, Luchon in France. The jersey is that of the GB team. More than 30 years later, few British riders have done better in the Tour de France than Robinson. Note the compressed-air pump clipped in front of his bottom bracket.

Right:

He was barrel-shaped when I met him and he was barrel-shaped when he was riding. Wim van Est looks ill at ease here, and the wavy chain suggests why. But few men laugh so much when the pressure's off.

Left:

Classic Bahamontes. High on the Galibier in 1964, back straight and upright, shorts eased up and slender thighs swelling.Note the names of riders scraped into the snow. Baha went on to win — 148 km in 7 h 20 min.

The Emperor, van Looy, at the height of his powers — a rainbow jersey on his back, Solo-Superia on his shorts, the rest of the race behind him. These were the days of handlebar gear controls and front pockets, but, uncharacteristically for the era, he has side-pull brakes.

Right:
Jan Derksen is older now, of course, and greyer. But in spirit he's still arm-aloft in an orange jersey. Here he's beating Maspes in the world championship semi-final at Rocourt, Belgium, in 1957.

Below:
The Lion of Flanders wins in the rain. This is the pro championship of 1956, and van Steenbergen is winning in Copenhagen. I've seen more judges at a club road race. The man on the line has his back to the race, perhaps to attend to the primitive photo-finish cam-era. *And why is the third rider already* sitting up?

Champion of the World, Graham Webb stands above Bernard Guyot (left) and a dejected René Pijnen, the home crowd's favourite at Heerlen in 1967. Webb lives now near Ghent in Belgium and drives a crane on the docks. His life has taken a turn for the better after reunion with his son.

Les gros bras — the big hitters of 1963. Anquetil crouches in bottom gear, Bahamontes sits upright in yellow, and Poulidor has a moment to check the peloton.

Master and servant. The grime, rain and pain of the 1969 Paris–Roubaix are etched into Hoban and Poulidor. The Englishman (left) had some of his finest rides with Poulidor's Mercier team.

Above:

Bottom gear and revving like fury, Charly Gaul nears the top of Mont Ventoux. It was a 21-km time trial in the 1958 Tour, and Gaul beat Bahamontes and Jean Dotto. It was close to this point, incidentally, that Tom Simpson died in 1967.

Left:

Poetry in motion. Long, lean legs, humped back, extended arms, sunken cheeks — it can only be Fausto Coppi. In those days chainsets were steel and cottered, and frames were tall and long.

Fausto Coppi was simply out training, according to the photographer's note. The thick tyres, casual shorts and no number suggest it is so. But marvel at the young girl's applause as he passes, and the fire in the face of the man in overalls.

Facing page:
A few short miles of time-trialling won Jan Janssen the Tour de France. It was the narrowest victory until Greg LeMond beat Laurent Fignon two decades later. Years afterwards, long-haired and off the back of the race, Janssen heard his name listed among the no-hopers on the race radio. It offended his pride and he brought his career to an end.

Above:
What would Barry Hoban have given for the Tour de France *maillot jaune*? This yellow jersey is from the Midi Libre of 1970. He complains that folk back home dismiss him as 'someone who once rode the Tour de France'.

Right:
Still in the characteristic dark glasses, Jan Janssen is back with his family just after winning the 1968 Tour de France on its last day. The bike he used still tours Holland for trade exhibitions, and Janssen is regularly called on to recall those days by Dutch television.

Even under pressure, Beryl Burton (*above*) looks more comfortable on the way to winning the world championship at Heerlen, Holland, than the officials crammed into the tiny following Volkswagen. Burton's bike has a small picture of Jacques Anquetil on the seat tube — he would have approved. *Right:* she would have won the men's BBAR if all her best rides had been in the same year. In 1962, time-trial officials were pedantically amateur-minded. Before this picture originally appeared after the 100-mile championship, the maker's name had to be inked out on the frame.

There's never a shortage of overweight men with vests and short legs to attend to riders in the Tour de France. Poulidor is — apart from getting a shower — moving up 49 seconds on the overall standings on the col du Grand St Bernard in 1966.

Ready for the attack. Bahamontes stocks up for the climb as Poulidor and Anquetil await the inevitable onslaught.

Below:

Were they genuine enemies, or thrown against each other by the papers? Either way, Poulidor and Anquetil never rode for the same trade team, never trusted the other on the road, and spoke of each other only wryly.

Right:
Shay Elliott was as cherubic as Stephen Roche but ultimately doomed. A career which included a world championship medal and Ireland's first yellow jersey ended in poverty, heartbreak and despair on the floor of his garage.

Raw roads and burning flesh in the 1953 Tour. *Above left:* the roads have improved since Oscar Lapize accused Henri Desgrange of trying to murder him, but the atmosphere is still there. No spectators watch Louison Bobet dodge the rocks, a spare tubular wrapped and knotted around his shoulders. *Above right:* Bobet has aluminium drinks bottles sealed with corks; the car passengers, probably journalists, look more like toffs off on a motoring holiday to Monte Carlo.

What would you give for a picture of yourself in this company? Joop Zoetemelk has Roger De Vlaeminck on his wheel and Jan Raas by his side. Eddy Merckx is behind Raas.

'I'd never suffered that much in my life before. I'd just done seven kilometres in the front and I was just having to hold these blokes.

'Everything came together 32km from the finish, and I decided halfway through the race that if we were together I should go away. Everyone went right for the bend and I went to the left, flat out.

'It may sound bigheaded but I knew I could ride faster than everyone else, even though I'd used so much. I was training 200–300km a day and the world championship was only 198km, so I was well within myself.

'I took 30 metres from that corner. I saw I had a gap and I knew I was world champion. There was another corner and 700 metres to go, and I thought if I can take the last corner without falling on my head, I was world champ.

'And it was one of the easiest races I'd ever ridden. Everything I'd planned happened. I crossed the line and the first thing I thought was "Were there only four blokes ahead of me? Were there more?" I put my arm in the air, but I thought "What have I done?"'

Next day, watching the pro race, he signed for Mercier. He wanted a French team anyway, but they also offered the best price. Little did he know, but his career was already over.

Mercier paid him as an amateur for the rest of the year and he spent the first weeks of winter training in Sardinia. A transport strike stopped him getting off the island, a phone strike stopped him telling Mercier. They still paid him but they weren't happy.

His first training bike fell to pieces, the toe-straps on his racing bike stretched uselessly in the *Het Volk* season-opener, and his knee started hurting unbearably in Kuurne–Brussels–Kuurne. His *soigneur* put him right for Paris–Nice the following week, but his French team-mates had lost interest by then.

They abandoned him at the end of the Paris–Nice prologue, and he had to leave his bike in a pub while a spectator gave him a lift, in his snow-soaked silk jersey, 40km to the team hotel. When he got there he ate his meal in silence and went for a massage.

'I went in and Poulidor was on the table with Stablinski sitting next to him, like at a confession. I said I'd come for my massage and they said "Get out — this is reserved for bike racers." So I went to sleep without a massage.'

From there on things went from bad to worse. His knee wracked him with pain, his bikes gave him endless trouble, and nobody wanted to know. By the end of the year he was very much the fallen idol, riddled with problems.

He had a small contract in Belgium, he made a kind of living, but it all ended about as quickly as it started.

The story doesn't end there, of course. He's national champion in Belgium, among the unlicensed riders who race like first-category riders in Britain but to whom nationality makes no difference. He had a little heart trouble, but apart from that he's fine. He's still a world champion to his neighbours.

He works on the docks in Ghent, where he reckons he's the best-paid crane driver in Belgium. Occasional British bike riders seek him out, and he welcomes that. He'd even do what he could for British bike teams — except he's never asked.

The thing that makes him really happy — apart from being at home and content and relaxed with life — is that his son is his son again. The two didn't speak for many years ... until one day he phoned out of the blue from Britain. The two of them were reconciled, father and son.

And that, beyond all his cycling triumphs, makes Graham Webb a happy man.

9 BARRY HOBAN (1940–)

There was a time when teachers would tell you that Belgium was bi-lingual. That's true only in the sense that it has two languages — or three if you count the protected German-speaking area near Liège. The reality is that you can draw a line east–west just south of Brussels and everyone below it will speak French and everyone above it, Dutch.

Neither speaks the other except as a foreign language, and more often than not the French-speaking Walloons don't speak Dutch at all. They dismiss it as a trivial, ugly provincial language which will never have the beauty or world status of French.

They may be right. Certainly they thought so when, a hundred years ago, the Walloons with their rich coal and steel industries dominated all Belgium and tried to squash out Dutch by the simple expedient of making it illegal to teach or print it.

The balance has now swung the other way. It is the north and its electronics industries that is rich; the south's coal and steel have gone the way of coal and steel everywhere in Europe. The bitterness of those French-dominated days remains, and Belgium has split into a federal state with separate governments for the north, the south and for the technically bi-lingual (but in practice French-speaking) capital.

Ghent is known to the Dutch speakers as Gent and to the Walloons as Gand. Antwerp, Liège, Kortrijk, Mechelen and Bruges, too, all have two names, and the signposts vary with the region you're in. Ghent, though, is an ancient capital, and there are still upper-class Flemings who would never consider themselves Walloons but who nevertheless speak only French.

Someone suggested once that Belgium could get round this problem by picking English as its national language instead — a neutral tongue causing no offence to either party. But since the French laugh at the Walloons' pronunciation, and the Dutch hear only yokels speaking when they listen to Flemings, the idea was abandoned when it seemed English would be merely a third language that Belgians would speak rather badly.

Had it happened, of course, it would have been a great help to the British and Irish riders in Ghent in particular. Nobody knows how many there are. Some live in hostels, others with families, and others — as the world pursuit champion Hugh Porter did once — in condemned flats with poor plumbing down by the docks.

In the 1960s, Ghent was the place for foreign adventurers. The police and public opinion allowed more races; cycling was still a sport which captured the public imagination. Tom Simpson lived at Mariakerke, on the city outskirts. Vin Denson had a bar in Ghent. Barry Hoban had his home there. And they made a golden era for island cycling. In fact, if there's one thing that depresses Barry Hoban, it's lack of recognition for what he did in those years. I upset him once and I was reminded of it sharply. Barry Hoban takes himself and his achievements seriously.

He won more stages of the Tour de France than Tom Simpson, more than Robert Millar or Brian Robinson … more than any Briton or Irishman before or since. But maybe because he was a sprinter, or perhaps because he lived his life in the shadow of the more spectacular Simpson, he's never ranked highly in public memory. In Britain, anyway.

It's no secret that it hurt when he returned from the Continent to a reception no more than lukewarm. There were no invitations to organise the national team; no requests to tour the country giving knowledge as a coach. He'd done his job, he'd earned his money, and nobody of importance thought he ought to do anything else. And so he was left with his bike, his suitcase, and a reputation for being no more than someone who once rode the Tour de France.

He has those who respect him and some who begrudge his success. He lives up a hillside in Wales, married to Simpson's widow Helen, and sells bike bits for a wholesaler.

'My one regret is not the question of money, although I could have made a lot of money today, but the fact that I am not known for what I did over there. No one knows who the hell Barry Hoban was. It would be nice to be known for what I did for the sport, and not pushed into oblivion as if it didn't count,' he says.

Like Tom Simpson, he moved to the Continent when cars were still loaded on ferries by crane and drivers with 'GB' or 'IRL' stickers were barons of the road.

'Cycling was the sport in Belgium. Everyone touched by the sport recognised you. You were someone. You could go into a shop in Ghent and everyone knew who you were.'

Not that Hoban is unimposing today. You have only to see him in his over-coat at a cycle show, not so much walking as progressing with some stateliness. I have a picture of Fausto Coppi doing much the same with Signor Campagnolo, and one might well have modelled himself on the other. Barry Hoban is aware of who he is.

And he has a view of how big riders ought to be treated, or at least how they used to be treated.

He told *Cycling* once: 'I remember to this day the first time that Jacques Anquetil actually spoke to me. Bear in mind that we were all professionals. The thing was that Anquetil spoke to me. You've got to realise that as a young kid just starting racing, Anquetil was already there. In the Tours of '56 and '57 I was a young teenager riding my bike, and guys like Anquetil were my time-trial heroes. There was an aura about those superstars which certainly isn't there today.

'They were larger than life and drove around in their big Mercedes cars. They always had, or seemed to have, super-glamorous attractive wives. There was always this film-star image about them — they aquaplaned above the ground and we were mere mortals who grovelled along.

'The *gros bras* we used to call them, the big arms. They were Anquetil, Altig, Stablinski, van Looy, all head and shoulders above everyone else. At a criterium, if we were eating beforehand, they would all eat together. We, the little lads, would all eat with our mates somewhere else.

'These guys were on a pedestal and were gentleman as well, compared to the antics of some riders today. They were always correct and a journalist's dream. The attitude was in being a real pro, and I can remember my manager looking me up and down at one team presentation, saying "Your jacket is very smart, but your trousers are too short."

'In the 60s you had superstars and they were on a pedestal. Even the other professionals looked up to them. We actually worshipped them. The difference then between the supertop riders and the ordinary good riders was enormous.'

On the other hand, he once criticised Eddy Merckx for being 'the biggest cry-baby in the business at the moment.'

'If he is beaten it is because of some mishap,' he said in 1967. 'If someone else wins then either Eddy would have won if he had been riding or the other man beat nobody, which is what he said when van Looy sprinted past me at Tours.

'I shall take great pleasure in outsprinting him one day next season, and then I shall tell him "Of course, Eddy, you've just been beaten by a nobody," just to remind him.'

If not for Merckx, then Hoban's admiration for Anquetil was such that he copied his toes-down riding, dismissed as brutal by stylists who preferred ankle-rotating smooth pedalling.

Hoban's career on the mainland lasted 18 years, first in France at Marles-les-Mines and then in Zomergem, near Ghent. They produced an odd record, with eight Tour de France stages but only one classic — and a classic at that, Ghent–Wevelgem, which has since lost its status by not being included in the World Cup. Perhaps that explains the curious view that people have taken of him since. For while Robinson pioneered, and Simpson drove himself senseless whenever he had the chance, Hoban peaked for the Tour de France and rocketed with his characteristically straight back out of the *peloton*. There were few long, lone breaks to glory or disaster, no duels hub-to-hub with winged eagles. Just a consistent ability to ride the last few miles, and sometimes just the last few hundred metres, faster than anybody else.

In those last few miles he snarled and snapped. He was, using the French word he favours, *électrique*. A colleague once said: 'Bloody hell! I thought you were a friend of mine. You don't want to know anyone towards the finish of a race, do you?'

He was a man who made his name in stage races, first the Tour of Spain and then the Tour de France.

His explanation: 'I could grovel to the finish, hit the hay and be like new the next day. I always went well towards the end of the Tour, and I would have loved it to go on for another week. I was never worn out at the end of the Tour.'

Barry and Helen Hoban live now above an industrial estate near Newport, Gwent. They moved in while he was working at the British Eagle factory at the bottom of the hill. He and the company parted when British Eagle, the oldest bike company in Britain, went bust and was bought from the liquidators by Townsend Cycles. But while he was there, a huge picture behind the receptionists' desk showed Tom Simpson as champion of the world.

It's not there under the new management and it's reasonable to assume that Hoban has it somewhere safe. So too is the scrapbook he kept when he began cycling and raced on a three-speed Daytona Flyer given him by his father. He joined the Wakefield Wheelers with no idea about racing, then rode an evening 10-miler run by the Calder Clarion. He finished in 27-40. And then came one of those curious links with the future and an association which would last the rest of his life.

His last race of his first year, at 16, is recorded in the scrapbook as 1-1-54 in the Scala Wheelers 25. The winner, in 57-14, was Tom Simpson. The association continued in the 1957 British League of Racing Cyclists hillclimb up Mam

Nick. Simpson won the senior title, Hoban was fourth in the junior. Next year Simpson came second and Hoban, now a senior, was seventh.

Simpson went abroad and Hoban followed in 1962. He arrived in Arras in the empty rolling hills of northern France on March 18 with another northerner, Bernard Burns. In those days a category of rider existed between the amateurs and professionals. Independents were supposed to be apprentice professionals, able to ride with amateurs or pros. In a couple of years they were to decide whether to turn pro or go back to the amateurs, but in practice — and especially in Britain where there were no professionals anyway — many just stayed independent and carved up the races between them. The toughness, even ruthlessness, of independent racing shouldn't be underestimated.

Hoban signed a contract with a cycle dealer called André Bertin to ride for Bertin Porter 39. It was worth 300 new francs a month. Porter 39 is a beer brand; Bertin had an affection for British riders because of his association with the characterful Harrogate dealer Ron Kitching, a pioneer of British road racing who had dabbled in the unknown world of Continental racing by sending a postal order to a foreign race organiser and asking to ride.

Kitching, who'd given Hoban some of his equipment in Britain, had been a mechanic in the Tour of Belgium. The team was managed by the Englishman Tommy Hill and included Albert Sercu, the father of six-day rider Patrick. Bertin sponsored the team, and Kitching and the Frenchman struck up a relationship which led to their appearing together on Bertin's stand at the 1948 Paris Show. It was from there that the Kitching wholesaling empire developed and made him a millionaire. He realised he had become a millionaire only when he sold the business and saw how many noughts were on the cheque that he poked under the grill of the bank.

Hoban said: 'I can only remember not being able to speak French for about two weeks. It was a case of sink or swim. We lived on omelettes for about the first 10 days because that was all we could recognise on the menu.'

Burns won his fourth race in France. But despite that, he returned to race in Britain as an independent for Falcon Cycles, the team for which Hoban also rode in his last years as a professional. But after a poor start, the man who stayed in France began to build a reputation for crafty riding.

He said afterwards: 'I had a damned good race sense, and later on in life I was called the Grey Fox, because they could never — no matter how old I was or supposedly how unfit — take it for granted that I wouldn't pull something off.

'I remember Géminiani saying "Listen, if you're not the strongest, you must be the craftiest."'

The French regional paper *La Voix du Nord* called him Public Enemy Number One, a title he enjoyed. It had been coined by riders that he beat.

'I was a bit of a crafty rider. I could weigh up the field pretty quickly. Only two guys could beat me in northern France in pure sprints — close sprints. I wondered how to beat them, so I gave them a hard ride. Once I got rid of them it was easy. I would go eyeballs out over the top and suddenly they weren't with us,' he told *Cycling*.

Public Enemy was an earned title. He won 16 races in his first season and had 50 placings in the first five. Next year he was even better.

'I always went for the race with the most money. I wasn't bothered about picking up bouquets or anything like that.'

He rode the Tour de l'Avenir in 1963, half an hour ahead of the Tour de France but with shorter stages. He won the bunch sprint on the Bordeaux track and finished 16th overall having seen the Pyrénées, the Alps and the Massif Central for the first time.

At this stage he could have turned professional for Pelforth, another French beer company. In time it was one of France's biggest teams, reaching its peak when Jan Janssen won the Tour de France in its yellow, white and blue on the last day. Pelforth also had a quiet Englishman called Alan Ramsbottom, another northerner, a man whose rimless glasses gave him the unjustified appearance of an *ingenue*. Ramsbottom is now a marathon runner back in England.

Hoban turned down the offer from Pelforth's manager, Maurice De Muer, to have another season with the amateurs and independents. He needed maturity and he realised it. Alongside both independents and pros, including Simpson, impetuosity denied him the opening stage of Paris–Luxembourg. He shot off, full of amateur enthusiasm, and blew up. He finished 10th overall nevertheless, and a distinct talent was appearing.

When he *did* turn, in 1964, he had a remarkable year: two stages in the Tour of Spain, one in the Midi-Libre, and his first ride in the Tour de France. It was the year of Anquetil's biggest duel with Poulidor.

'In those days it was almost like folklore. I would have paid to have ridden my first Tour,' says Hoban.

Whether he sees himself as a sprinter — he's always spoken of himself as an all-rounder, but it was from sprinting that most of his victories came — he had the novelty in 1965 of riding the biggest of the sprinters' classics.

The organisers of Paris–Tours were tired of claims that their race was boring because of the massed sprints which always ended them. The country south of Paris is gentle and undemanding, and pretty soon the race acquired a reputation for favouring sprinters, or for nothing happening until the last hour, or for being won on a particular hill. Paris–Tours was a sprinters' race, declining as non-sprinters looked elsewhere in frustration.

And so the promoters hit on their idea.

'It is the derailleur gear that has spoiled our race. We have no mountains, no severe climbs. Gears just push the speeds higher and higher until the race is nullified. From now on gears will be banned and *coureurs* will ride as they did in the sport's glory days, on single freewheels,' they announced.

It was a folly.

In the old days riders had to leap off and reverse their back wheels, using the larger or smaller sprocket on the other side of the hub. But hubs had become single-sided since those days, with what used to be a second thread smoothed off. It proved impossible to find enough wheels which fitted the old way of doing things, so Paris–Tours allowed one front chainring and a freewheel with three sprockets.

Hoban recalled in *Cycling*: 'Our team manager Antonin Magne, the star of the Thirties, was in heaven. It was back to his era and all his talk was of his big gear of 49 ˘ 15. For the 1965 event I used 51 ˘ 14, 15, 16, starting with the 16 sprocket, and I never had time or was too scared to jump off and change as no one was hanging around. We in the Mercier-BP team had not thought this one out and the only way to get back was to rev even more.

'There was no question of dropping to the 13 to get back quickly, as Jacques Anquetil found out. He started with 52 ˘ 14 and in the valley of the Chevreuse he found the going hard. He jumped off and put a smaller gear in, but made no impression on the bunch at first. Then two of his Ford France team-mates went back to assist, then six more, then the whole team.

'When he eventually got back, Jean Stablinski played hell with him.'

Did it slow the race? No, it did not. Hoban changed gear only once in the 1965 and 1966 events, and Gerben Karstens of Holland won at 45.029kmh on a 53 ring with 14, 15 and 16 sprockets. After 50 kilometres, Karstens' whole team jumped off at the same time and switched to 14.

The experiment was abandoned, having proved nothing.

In 1967, Hoban won his first Tour stage. It was the day after Simpson died on Mont Ventoux, and those who were there remember events differently. What they agree on is that they decided, after a mixed vote, to stay in the race. They agree too that Jean Stablinski put the view of the rest of the race that a Briton should win at Sête. The question mark is over who was intended to win.

Vin Denson insists that it should have been him, that he was nominated because he was Simpson's closest friend. On the other hand, he concedes that he did not take the opportunity immediately.

Hoban said: 'I was just riding along and suddenly I was by myself.'

In his book *Watching the Wheels Go Round*, he says he would have preferred Colin Lewis or Arthur Metcalfe to have won. He concedes that it changed his career tremendously, that he felt he had taken over from Simpson 'as British cycling ambassador on the Continent'.

The first proper stage win came at Sallanches after 18 days in 1968. It followed second place on day eight, from Royan to Bordeaux, then third next day at Bayonne.

Sallanches was an extraordinary win for a man remembered as a sprinter. The road that separated Grenoble from Sallanches was 200km long and decorated with five mountains. It also ended on the Cordon, above Sallanches. Hoban rode clear on the drop to Albertville, allowed his lead by a pacific bunch just as Brian Robinson had been earlier.

By Hery he had 10 minutes, then eight minutes at the foot of the Aravis, where he won a £200 prime in honour of the cantankerous and sockless Henri Desgrange, the race's founder.

The lead fell to seven and then six minutes but he kept it to the finish. The following year, 1969, he won two more stages on successive days, at Bordeaux and Brive, and his name was made. If not among the real stars, then at least he was a regular winner, a man who could never be overlooked.

The Grey Fox had struck.

In 1973 came two more wins, the second after a puncture with 20 kilometres to go. The mechanic made a quick wheel-change, and — not thinking it important — tightened the quick-release on the left rather than the right. The difference is no more than cosmetic, but it bothered Hoban and he jumped off and turned the wheel. Doubtless the team-mates who paced him back to the bunch with four kilometres left had an opinion on the extra hold-up.

Hoban reached the first 10 riders on the last bend, 350 metres from the line. He didn't so much sprint as continue his pursuit, going round Jacques Esclassan and Belgium's Staf van Roosbroeck and holding them off.

It had been a tough day and he slept well. Next morning came news that he had been caught for doping. Hoban insisted he had taken only a cold treatment on the rainy stage to Nice; the boffins analysed the sample again and pronounced it negative.

Grey hair was showing when Hoban rode the Tour for the last time, in 1978. A youngster called Bernard Hinault had just started, and insiders hinted he was a guy to look out for. At Germigny l'Evêque, in 1980, Hoban won his last race and came back to Britain.

Times have changed since then. They have moved on without Hoban. He never managed a pro team here or on the Continent. He never became national coach or team manager. There are a dozen views on why that should be, but all that matters in the end is that it didn't happen.

'Pro teams then were a million miles behind in organisation compared to teams today. Exceptionally they would take an extra mechanic to the Tour de France, and exceptionally they would take two *soigneurs* for the tours. These guys were eyeballs out just looking after you. Nowadays they have four mechanics, four *soigneurs*, and basically you've got one *soigneur* looking after two guys,' he told *Cycling*. 'In my days one *soigneur* would look after five guys. The team leaders were looked after, and by the time they got to someone like me it was just a cat's lick. They were too smashed to give you a good rub.

'In my days there were no clipless pedals, no concealed brakes. Today's riders don't ride at 28mph all the time. Why, the record for Paris–Roubaix has been held by Peter Post since 1964. That was ridden at 28mph.

'What I did from 1962 to 1980, it's as though it didn't count. I know when I go back to the Continent it's like the return of the prodigal son. I go to the Ghent Six and straight away everyone says "Ah, Barry's here."

'They say hello to me on the microphone. I say hello to Patrick Sercu, and all the mechanics say "Ah, Barry's come back again." I was walking around the centre of the Ghent Six and people were coming up to me who were only kids when I was racing there. It's a nice feeling.

'Over here it's "So you rode the Tour a few years ago; so what?"'

10 RIK VAN STEENBERGEN (1924–)

It wasn't easy to see Rik van Steenbergen. To start with, he has an ex-directory phone number, which I had to get in dubious circumstances. And second, there's the matter of football.

I was back in Antwerp, a complicated city where damned souls can be doomed to ride for ever on cobbled streets with round-nosed trams. I wanted a hotel which didn't advertise quite so blatantly that it was open all 24 hours. Those signs, and the girls in their tight, short minis, led to conclusions. So did the realisation that in Antwerp you are never that far from the docks.

So I booked into a posher hotel than I'm accustomed to, left my bike in a garage, and phoned van Steenbergen from reception. The manager realised quickly who I was talking to and listened in attentively.

'Come tomorrow evening but come before eight,' the old warrior said. 'And watch out for the dog. He's harmless but he terrifies people.' I said I would do both, and he stressed again the importance of getting there on time. 'At eight o'clock there's a big match on television and I want to watch Belgium play.'

I said in that case I'd be sure to be there earlier.

As it turned out, the village was further out than I'd bargained for, and I'd also made several circuits of those hellish back streets. So I was late. The other instructions were to ring him again from the village centre and he'd direct me to Mandalay Lane, where he lives.

I pushed a dull five-franc coin into the callbox slot and dialled his number. It rang four times.

'*Ja?*'

'*Daag* ... it's Les Woodland.'

'I told you to come before eight, *meneer*. It's five past.'

'Sorry ...'

'And the match has started ...'

'Sorry ...'

'Come back tomorrow, *hé?*'

I came back tomorrow and found that Mandalay Lane was half a mile out-side the village, a turning from a straight road that led into an avenue of trees and posh detached houses. I wasn't looking forward to facing him.

I took it slowly until I found his number. It was a large white house, with castle-like turrets, like a Moorish palace. The double gates were open and van Steenbergen, cuddly, grey-haired and avuncular, came down the steps from the front door as I arrived. There was no sign of the fierce dog.

'Call me Rik,' he said, which is charmingly informal by Belgian standards. Dutch, like French, lends itself to formality. Rik van Looy did not ask me to call him Rik. But then it soon emerged that Rik van Steenbergen would gladly be .everything that Rik van Looy isn't.

'I always tried to get on with him, but it never happened. He saw me as the man he had to beat and there has always been a coolness between us. We have never been friends. I have invited him to my own race, the Grote Prijs van Steenbergen, so I have tried, but I do not think we will ever get on,' he said.

A large picture in his front room shows his glory days. The room is tasteful, the settee comfortable. There are books and pictures and a television. He's wear-ing a red Solo shirt. For a while, the two Riks were in the same team. There are certificates on the wall marking his world championships. He won in 1949, 1956 and 1957. He was third in 1946. He was also Belgian champion in 1943, 1945 and 1954.

We drank coffee together. This wasn't the grumpy man who answered the phone and told me to go away. This was a charming *patron*, an elder statesman, with a smile and a laugh. He still works part-time, selling verandas or somesuch. To my surprise — because you don't expect such things of Lions of Flanders who have fought their way through the flying grit and rain of northern Belgium — his wife comes from Wigan. She speaks English with a mixture of Wigan and Flemish accents. van Steenbergen goes to Wigan with her once or twice a year; they walk around the shops and the houses, and nobody, presumably, knows who the heck they are. When one of the clubs there discovered it, they had the wit to invite van Steenbergen to their annual dinner. I have no idea whether he accepted.

His wife has been his saviour.

'When I stopped racing, I knew nothing. There was nothing for me to do. I had been a racing cyclist. Now there was nothing. I should have stopped slowly, but I didn't. It was very sudden, and there was a gap in my life. And I fell into bad company,' he told me.

He'd go drinking and playing cards and living the sort of life that's safe and permissible when you're 17 but dangerous when you're 42 with a fair bit of money, no wife to keep you in order and a lot of time to kill. I called it his black period and he didn't dispute it.

In fact, when I said 'and there was a black period in your life, wasn't there?', what I was hinting at was the widespread belief that he'd once been locked in clink for breaking into a chemist's shop and stealing drugs. There was no point in hinting because he didn't pick up on it. In the end I had to ask him straight out — 'Weren't you in jail once?'

I felt about as comfortable as I had when I asked Peter Post if he'd been in the habit of fixing races.

van Steenbergen thought it a huge joke.

'Good grief, no!' he roared, and he slapped his thigh. 'I was never in jail. What a story that would have made in the papers — van Steenbergen in jail! No, one of those that I fell in with was involved with something like that and the police went round interviewing everybody he knew. And they knew I was one of his friends, and I went down to the police station and answered their questions, but I was never a suspect and I was never in jail!'

His wife had no idea she'd met one of Belgium's greatest racing cyclists, and that, perhaps, made their union all the sweeter.

Rik van Steenbergen was born in Arendonk, a few miles away, on September 9, 1924. He turned professional, for what that meant then, while Belgium was still occupied by the Germans in 1943. He was only 19 — too young to turn professional without the benefit of a forged German identity card.

The Germans believed — or at least the French-speaking southern Belgians believe they believed — that the northern Flemings were more Germanic and therefore deserving of better treatment. There were still bike races in wartime Flanders, although usually with prizes in kind rather than money. It's also undeniable that some northern Belgians (and possibly some southerners as well) also considered themselves sufficiently Germanic to co-operate more than they should.

When the Canadians liberated the Antwerp area in 1945, there were many Belgians who either found themselves with money they had earned dubiously or wanted to patronise local events to rehabilitate themselves before accusations were made.

It was then that Belgium became a place to earn big money on a bike with few irksome regulations. Schoolboys and juniors raced with adults. There were absurd primes outside the shop of any businessman who cared to offer them. There were races of all distances for whoever wanted to ride. And a disappointing but astute fair-haired track rider called Jan van Buggenhout saw his chance.

There were so many races that the best had difficulty deciding which to ride and with whom to negotiate. And organisers competed for riders good enough to draw paying spectators and sponsors. More than that, cyclists were rarely bright or good at negotiating, given their backgrounds as farm labourers or factory workers.

van Buggenhout made the grade as an agent when he got van Steenbergen as his client. He used him as a bargaining point with everyone he met. Within a few years he was not only controlling Belgian domestic racing but running a whole circuit of round-the-houses village races.

van Steenbergen never again lacked a pocketful of francs. He was superb in round-the-houses races. He was good in fast finishes: he won the Giro d'Italia in 1951, along with 15 stages. And he was good enough at single-day classics to win Milan–San Remo in 1954 and come second in 1959, win the Tour of Flanders in 1944 and 1946, Paris–Roubaix in 1948 and 1952, and Paris–Brussels in 1950.

But the mountains were a mystery to him and, wisely, he stuck to the winter tracks in preference to summer climbs. He won more six-days than anyone before him.

He was 15 when war broke out. His family was poor and ate little more than unbuttered bread. He should have been disqualified in his first junior race, the Circuit of Flanders, but the judges dismissed him as a no-hoper whom it would do no harm to encourage. They let him continue. To their surprise, and perhaps their dismay, he won the hills championship, the time-trial, the last stage — and first place overall.

Years later, something similar happened when Eddy Merckx was disqualified in his first race after finishing so far ahead that the judges couldn't be convinced he hadn't cheated.

This junior success continued in his first professional race, which he also won. It came again when he won Paris–Roubaix at a record 43.6kmh, admittedly helped by a tailwind.

In 1952, the world was more nationalistic. There were moves towards European unity, but the continent still stood scarred from the war and tended to grievances. Holland had been bombed out of neutrality ... Belgium became the war's unwilling cockpit ... France was divided under Pétain ... Germany was the aggressor ... and so on.

van Steenbergen was Belgium's hope after yet another wartime battering, and there were crowds at races the like of which — like football matches in England — have never been seen since. Unfortunately, van Steenbergen was at sea in the major tours, good for four stages in France and six in Spain, but a hopeless bet for overall victory.

By contrast, Italy and France had the aces in Fausto Coppi and Bobet. Belgium demanded van Steenbergen prove himself against the *vedettes* and he knew it.

So when he came to the start at St-Denis in Paris for the ride to Roubaix, he had more than a little on his mind. Apart from anything else, there was the need to win something big to keep up his contract price — and one suspects that contract prices were important to van Steenbergen.

What made life more exciting is that Coppi had much the same idea. He had little chance of winning in a sprint; it had to be alone, and the cart tracks and the abandoned farm roads of the last sixty miles should give him scope enough.

'Keep up the speed,' Coppi ordered his team. 'It's our only chance. We've got to weaken the sprinters on their own ground.' The needles in the following cars crept upwards as Coppi put on the pressure. He sent his team-mates away repeatedly to wear out what he believed could be a sizeable number of wheel-suckers who might come by in the last miles and leave him.

And then Coppi made his own move. As best he could — because he was too light to make a harsh attack — he accelerated to a point where only three riders could stay with him. Kübler was there, and Dupont and Baldassari, clinging to him in hope.

It was easier then to find the cobbles which make the race's reputation. It's always said that the rough roads are a continuous feature of the last third of the course, but it's never been so. It would be remarkable if the organisers could string together so many roads that were never intended to link more than fields or hamlets.

So, when Coppi had established his break, he could ease a little on a brief road stretch knowing that the chasers were still on the cobbles and potholes behind. A pause gave him the chance to gather his wits and his breath before dismissing the three challengers on the next stretch of cobbles. They, too, knew it was about to happen.

But Coppi had scarcely caught his breath when a great commotion started behind him. From nowhere came the roar of motorcycles and the blowing of whistles and hooters. He looked round just in time to see the giant body of van Steenbergen hurtling not simply towards him but straight by as well.

'The Belgian was riding like a possessed man,' Coppi recalled. 'It was like seeing a pursuiter coming up to me. He was crouched over his bike as if there were only four kilometres to ride. It was unbelievable.'

Coppi leaped onto the pedals and set off after him. They held each other for a while in armed truce, and then Coppi attacked with 15 miles to go. It was a scarring, searing attack. Dupont was shot off, Baldassari vanished, and finally the great Swiss, Kübler, could hold on no longer. Two of the greatest riders in the world — the wiry, inexhaustible Coppi and the powerful, more vulnerable van Steenbergen. Both were streaked in sweat and congealed mud and dust. You couldn't have a better billing.

van Steenbergen could win the sprint, and he knew it. But there was no guarantee that Coppi could not get a few metres' lead and, having got it, ride an epic solo to the cycle track at Roubaix. Equally, Coppi knew he could stay away, but was far from convinced that the Belgian would let him. He had to attack him over and over again, to weaken him, to make his sprint impotent and thereby profit either on the track or, better still, on the flat roads to the stadium.

Grippingly, van Steenbergen had the same thoughts. Coppi attacked five times, and five times van Steenbergen held him. Each time, the Belgian was forced to climb out of the saddle like a great road sprinter and struggle for a mile to cover the handful of metres that separated him from the shelter of Coppi's wheel.

'I knew at that moment that I had lost Paris–Roubaix,' Coppi told *Gazette della Sport* reporters. 'I had done what I could but I could not budge him.'

Coppi reached a thin brown arm into the back pocket of his jersey and took a swig from a bottle. The pair swung onto the track and, predictably, van Steenbergen won Paris–Roubaix.

Diplomatically, he confessed: 'If Coppi had attacked just once more, I'd have been lost.'

Coppi laughed.

'If he'd have eased up a mite, I would have attacked,' he said.

A few moments later, André Mahé arrived as third man.

van Steenbergen never won the race again. It wasn't his last success. He was still good for the world championship in 1956 and 1957 (in Waregem, Belgium, where he was received by King Baudouin). And, of course, he rode the track. All year round, van Steenbergen was a draw, earning money. He won 1,591 races on the track.

Go now on the motorway north out of Antwerp towards Breda in Holland, and on the right, below the elevated section, is a curiously shaped building like a beached whale. The roof is rounded, the curved brick walls still painted with fading advertisements for a newspaper that went out of existence a decade and more ago.

You find it by turning off the motorway at Merksem and going back on yourself so that you park under the elevated road. The car park was pitted and puddled when I went to pay tribute. They've changed the inside now and fitted bright plastic seating and modern lights. But for years the giant indoor velodrome was dark and draughty, the wooden seats and barriers stained by decades of cigar smoke and spilt beer. There was an ice rink under the track centre, holes in the roof that allowed the snow to fall through, and when it got too bad the riders tackled the last hour of the Antwerp Six in tracksuit tops.

And it was on this sad but nostalgic track — so large that the six-day was ridden by teams of three — that Rik van Steenbergen said goodbye on December 10, 1966. The Sportpaleis put on a celebration night for him and 20,000 people turned up to wish him well.

I assume that many people still feel the same way. It's probably one reason the telephone number at the villa in Zoersel remains ex-directory.

11 FAUSTO COPPI (1919–1960)

The world's divided over who was its greatest rider. But make a brief list and the man who fought with van Steenbergen on the road to Roubaix will always be one of the top three.

In one of the many books commemorating Coppi, a director of the newspaper *La Gazette della Sport* writes in the closing pages: 'I pray that the good God will one day soon send us another rider like Coppi.'

Coppi, to Italians after the war, was a symbol of Italy's liberation. A nation confused at fighting on both sides, a simple folk to whom the city fascists must have seemed an attractive but mysterious puzzle, found its roots in Coppi. There is, in the Italian culture, a wish to identify with humble peasants making bread and hanging their washing on lines behind shambly, sun-bleached hovels.

You won't get Italians to live there, of course — Italians are as fond as anyone else of running water, sanitation, comfortable beds and reliable electricity — but it is in the peasant culture that Italy, like France, finds its heart and identity.

Coppi, a man discovered at the hands of a blind masseur, held prisoner by the British during the war and then returned to dominate, only to shatter his bones in that domination, was all that Italy needed.

That the angel should fall to earth in a sex scandal and then die prematurely simply made the legend complete.

While he was at his peak, half Italy would gather around medium-wave radio sets and wait for Mario Ferretti to announce the inevitable: 'There is just one man in the lead.' And then: 'It's Coppi …'

If you doubt this enthusiasm, ponder this: at a time when Italy lay in ruins and hungry men caught chickens in the street, there were four daily papers dedicated solely to sport. Such a paper has never succeeded in Britain, Ireland or almost anywhere else.

What fuelled their success and kept ears on the radio was the eternal tussle between Coppi and Gino Bartali, a laconic-looking man known as the Pedalling Monk. The Vatican is enclosed by Italy, but that doesn't make Italy a Catholic country. One in two Italians were at one time Communists, and you don't get many Communists at mass.

Bartali was devoted to the church, Coppi rather less so. In fact Coppi was probably an atheist, although he was wise enough never to commit himself. At the peak of Coppi's adultery scandal, the Pope refused to bless a *peloton* while he remained in it. It would be as difficult to imagine the Pope denying Bartali as it would be to imagine Bartali being in similar circumstances in the first place. You could no more support Coppi *and* Bartali than you could favour both the Rolling Stones and the Beatles in the sixties. Coppi was Jagger to Bartali's McCartney.

Country folk backed Bartali; townies were Coppi fans, attracted by his progressive ways and, at the same time, by his traditional peasant background. There is a story — and here you have to remember that many Coppi stories are merely legends — that Gino Bartali once sneaked into Coppi's hotel room to search his suitcase for what made him ride so well. The problem is distinguishing the truth from the wild invention, but on stories like that the fanaticism and rivalry of Italian fans bred.

Bartali might date his eclipse back to January 7, 1940. He sat then in a house in Milan, with an elderly man smoking a pipe. Eberrardo Pavesi was himself a former rider, but by 1940 he had become manager of the Legnano team. He'd been signing riders to support Bartali, who had his eyes on the Giro d'Italia. Bartali always called him Father.

As Pavesi lowered his pipe and blew smoke into the room in a stream, he said almost by-the-by that he had signed Fausto Coppi as a *domestique*. Bartali rarely queried the Father's views. He thought for a while. His worry wasn't that Coppi was too strong, rather that he might be too weak. Bartali was a marked man among even the Italian riders after winning the Tour de France in 1938, the last before war broke out. He needed strength behind him.

Coppi showed it on the Giro's first day. Bartali crashed and Coppi stayed behind to help. But a week later, after a succession of attacks which left all the Legnano team save Coppi and Bartali out of touch, it was clear that this Fausto was a man in contention.

That night, at the team dinner, Pavesi announced: 'I've reshuffled the team. From now on, Magni and Favalli, you will be *domestiques*. And Coppi is to be a favoured rider.' Bartali stayed team captain, but Coppi was pretender to his throne.

And so it might have stayed had Coppi not bloodied his sword on the last stage. On the climb of the Abetone, he set off in pursuit of the breakaway — Vicini and Valetti. Nobody could live with him. Within moments Coppi was alone and soaring.

Stabbed in the back, Bartali shouted at the rest of the team and they set off in angry pursuit. But the whole Legnano force was no match. Coppi finished alone, four minutes ahead on general classification, and took the pink jersey of leadership. Bartali never forgave him and spent the rest of his career seeking revenge.

On November 7, 1942, Coppi broke the hour record on the Vigorelli in Milan. Then he left for Tunisia to fight for Italy. His best pal was a man called Chiappucci. Decades later, the man's son, Claudio, by then an Italian road star of the 1990s, said: 'Do you know why I picked cycling? Because my dad fought the second world war alongside Fausto Coppi. They ate together out of the same plate.'

Coppi's was a brief war. Montgomery's army captured him within months and he spent the rest of the conflict in a prisoner-of-war camp. Few among the British soldiers who held him knew or cared who he was, although Coppi spoke well of the way he was treated.

The British put him eventually on a ship for Italy, and from there he took a train to Naples. He wore his Italian soldier's trousers, a British army jacket and a German cap. And he was hungry. As he left the station, a voice called his name. He turned wearily and recognised Adolfo Leoni, another demobbed soldier, who'd been lodging since his release with a local cycle dealer. The shopkeeper, a man called Nulli, had been organising local races with what he could collect from spectators as prizes.

Coppi started to regain some of his enthusiasm, although his health was harder to find. When he was ready, he signed for Bianchi. It was the start of the most legendary pairing in the sport.

Eduardo Bianchi opened his small bicycle factory in 1884. The bicycle boom was brief, though, and a few years later he followed the trend and began making cars and motorcycles as well. Even so, things still weren't an immediate success and he began looking for publicity. He backed another trend and decided to sponsor racing cyclists.

His first success was in 1911: the team prize in the Giro d'Italia. He signed Alfredo Binda, the three-time world champion who gave his name to toestraps used for decades afterwards, and for years he and the bosses of Legnano quarrelled over the best riders in the world.

Bianchi stayed loyal even when sponsorship became more expensive and the *extra-sportifs* joined the sport. The name stayed on the jerseys, smaller now and secondary to Carpano, then Campagnolo and later to Faema, the coffee machine company — but it remained.

There were gaps, admittedly. There were no Bianchis in the bunch from 1959 to 1964 or from 1967 to 1972. But when the stars rode, they rode Bianchi — Géminiani, Petrucci, Adorni, Baronchelli, Adorni, all rode Bianchis.

How many bikes they and Coppi sold through their exploits is anybody's guess, but the publicity was enormous.

On May 19, 1946, Coppi arrived at the start of Milan–San Remo in his pale blue Bianchi jersey. It was a day to savour. He attacked almost from the start and took five riders with him. He began the climb of the Turchino with the only one who could hold him, Lucien Teissiere, and by the top he was alone.

He was pleased to have done it, but it wasn't his plan. At that stage, the most marked man in the race, he was still 150km from the finish. And the roads ahead of him were not simply lengthy but scarred and at times barely ridable because of the war.

Whichever way he thought of it, it wasn't pleasant. He'd realised on the climb that he didn't fancy hours of constant sparring with Teissiere and he had repeatedly attacked him. And Teissiere, who was by no means over-awed by his company, attacked back. On the other hand, the only other option was to sit it out in the bunch and wait for a mass sprint that he, a relatively poor sprinter, was unlikely to win. Milan–San Remo is usually decided on the Poggio climb, half an hour or so before the finish, and it's doubtful that anybody who'd witnessed him go away on the Turchino was likely to give him the same privilege again.

And so he went on alone.

A mass of official and journalists' cars swept up to him, pushing the unfortunate Teissiere further back with their breeze.

At San Remo, Coppi had 14 minutes. The break, first with companions, then with Teissiere — whose exploits are still considered legendary in Italy — and finally alone, had lasted 270 kilometres. Teissiere finished four and a half minutes ahead of the bunch, which meant that Coppi had beaten Bartali by 18 minutes.

There are too many stories of Coppi to tell them all. In 1952 the organisers of the Tour de France had a first prize and a bonus for whoever came second. That the winner would be Coppi was inevitable. Without an attractive second prize, there was little for the rest to dispute.

He dominated the race so much that when a minnow called Jacques Vivier won a stage he turned to reporters to say: 'I thank Mr Coppi that he allowed me to win this stage in front of my own people. Mr Coppi is a gentleman, but he is far too strong for us.'

The biggest post-war winning margin is Coppi's 28 minutes 27 seconds in 1952, ahead of Stan Ockers. There's no such official title as *campionissimo*, but by consent there have been only four champion of champions: Constante Girardengo, Alfredo Binda, Gino Bartali, and Coppi.

An old black-and-white film called *Of Sport and Men* shows Coppi in an unknown race, possibly the Tour de France. It's a long, hard climb, and two dozen riders are strung in a line on his wheel.

You see Coppi's lean calves, the oily floppy hair, the hunched back, the beaky nose like a rudder. He is on his smaller ring, pedalling quickly but not fast. A musette hangs round his shoulders and, with one arm on his handlebars and the other groping the small of his back, he is ferrying food to his jersey pockets.

Two, three, four times Coppi reaches into the musette. Then, sure of his food, he places his second hand alongside the first, pulls harder on the handlebars, and rides away. The sequence is no more than four minutes long. But they are the most gripping minutes you'll see. They were archetypical, too, of a man who needed to ride that way because he had no sprint to talk of. Apart from Milan–San in 1946, he had eight minutes in hand after riding from Alpe d'Huez to Serestrière across the Alps in the 1952 Tour de France.

Just before he died, Coppi rode at Herne Hill. His greatest years were behind him. And yet those acres were crammed not just by cyclists but by Italian Londoners, men in suits, men in dungarees, men who screamed and wept for their idol.

For where Hinault created fear, Anquetil admiration and Merckx respect, Coppi gained worship — and, occasionally, hatred.

His career has a *Boy's Own* quality: the humble boy whose mother didn't like him playing in the cold, discovered by a blind masseur who predicted his future. For, as the story has it, Biaigio Cavanna guided Coppi with his words and touch to world championships and the world hour record. In 1949 and 1952, Coppi won the Tour and the Giro in the same year. He won five Giros, two Tours de France, five Tours of Lombardy, four Italian titles, three Milan–San Remos, four Barrachi Trophy time-trials, the 1947 and 1949 world pursuit championships, the 1953 world road championship and, in 1942, the world hour record in 45.871km.

The street where he lived as a boy is now named after him. You can find it for yourself. You start at the top of the boot of Italy, in Genoa, then take the main road almost due north towards Milan. Midway between the cities, the motorway swings left to bypass a town still served by the old road. The town is Tortona and it's there, after the First World War, that Coppi ran errands on his bike for the butcher.

Nearby, 15 miles away, is Coppi's own village of Castellania. There were only 300 people there when Coppi was born on a farm outside Castellania on September 15, 1919, and many were his relatives. An uncle who went to sea and became a captain bought young Fausto a specialised racing frame when he came home on shore leave, and so a legend began. In recognition, the Giro passed through Castellania in silence in 1989.

Go right through the town and at the end you'll find the family house. It's in Via Fausto Coppi.

He married Bruna Ciampolini but, although they had a daughter, it was not a happy marriage. He was also more and more afflicted by broken bones. You'd never look at Coppi and say, as you might of Seb Coe or Eddy Merckx or Muhammad Ali, that here was a man built for athletic greatness. Even when he rode, there was no transformation into poetry on wheels. He was round-shouldered, like many of his generation who trained only by riding a bike and never considered their posture; his face was cadaverous, his legs lean and twig-like.

And the unhappier he became with Bruna, and the more frequently he rose to a peak only to be brought down by broken bones, the more he began to lose faith in himself. According to those who raced with him, including the Dutchman Wim van Est, it was then, around 1949, that he began in a big way to use what was then called 'scientific preparation.'

This isn't to devalue his achievements. He was doing — using amphetamine — no more than his rivals. In fact, in *Sporting Cyclist* he used reporter René de la Tour to warn Italian amateurs against 'using bombs.'

And in this decline of confidence, he fell in love with the so-called *Dama Bianca*, the Woman in White, the woman next door. He abandoned his wife — Catholic law would not allow them a divorce — and moved in with her. And fans who once struggled to touch his clothing spat on him as he passed. She, by the way, must have had a name. But you rarely see it. She's simply the *Dama Bianca*, because whenever the Italian tabloids saw her, she was wearing white. Simple.

If you ever stay on a campsite with Italians during the world championship, you will find them ecstatic or suicidal by turns. Ecstasy precedes the championship, which of course Italy will win; depression follows when the *azzuri* fail to do the business. Bearing this in mind, you can see why Italy turned against the unhappy Coppi. Bartali fans were convinced they had been right all along; Coppi followers felt betrayed.

The Pope refused to bless the Giro d'Italia because it included the now scandalous adulterer.

Slowly the career flickered. Coppi's mistake, perhaps, was not to have given up. He was 20 when he won the Giro d'Italia for the first of five times, but 30 when he rode his first Tour de France and 33 when he won it for the last time. Perhaps it was the feeling that in this, as in love and health, he had been cheated by time and fate that made him keep going. He certainly didn't need the money. In 1957, when he was rider-manager of a young Coppi-Carpano team, his saintly status had faded enough for income-tax officials to start prodding into his affairs. The amounts, after all these years, seem minuscule. Twelve pounds would have been a good weekly wage. But Coppi, remember, had been the world's best-paid racing cyclist.

Quite what he put on his tax forms nobody knows. But it was less, considerably less, than the officials reckoned he *should* have put down. They claimed that in 1955 and 1956 he earned something like £50,000; that he owned estates and farms, a razor-blade factory and interests in two cycle factories. They said that he received £15,000 for linking his name with Carpano. Even after his peak, they said, he was getting £500 for a track appearance.

Now disillusioned, he rode an exhibition race in 1959 at Ouagadougou in Upper Volta, West Africa, with Roger Rivière, Henry Anglade (known as Napoleon in the *peloton* because of his authoritarian views), Jacques Anquetil, Roger Hassenforder ('the pedalling clown') and Raphaël Géminiani. Then he went on safari in the Porga game reserve. He was tired and there were bags under his eyes. Shooting was his favourite relaxation. The date was December 13, 1959.

Five days later, Coppi returned to Europe seriously ill. He was joined by Raphaël Géminiani, who also felt unwell. The others followed two days afterwards. Coppi and Géminiani said farewell at Orly Airport in Paris and started off again for his home at Novi-Ligure.

He had been home for two days when he began vomiting and running a temperature. In Clermont-Ferrand, Géminiani was doing the same.

An ambulance took Coppi to the hospital in Tortona. He now had pains in his back and chest. They put him in an oxygen tent and watched the graphs ticking off his temperature at more than 40 degrees and his heart at 180 — about the same as it would have been in the most arduous climbs of the Alps. Malaria wasn't untreatable, but his condition was worsened by a preliminary diagnosis that he had no more than flu.

Monsignor Ferrerazzo, a priest, administered the last rites.

At 8.45 on the morning of January 2, 1960, Coppi died. He was 40. His obituary ran to two pages in *L'Equipe* and considerably longer in *La Gazzette della*

Sport. Anquetil, Bobet, Rivière and Bartali were among the 10,000 people at his funeral at Castellania.

In Clermont-Ferrand, Géminiani made a slow recovery lasting several months. He did get back to racing, but at the foot of the col de l'Escrinet, in the Dauphiné–Libéré, he climbed off his bike for good. He lives now in Provence, in the same village as the Belgian rider and former television commentator, Fred De Bruyne.

If you climb the hill in Castellania to the church, you'll find four copper poles in the graveyard. They're three feet high, the height it needs to list Coppi's achievements. Alongside him is his brother Serse, also a racing cyclist, who died after crashing onto a pavement in the 1953 Tour of Piedmont. By the time Fausto arrived at the hospital Serse had died, and for a while Fausto was all for abandoning cycling. He returned only because Bianchi's commercial director persuaded him that riding the Tour de France was 'the best way to forget.'

Alongside Fausto's grave is a marble urn with bags of earth brought there from the biggest mountains of the Tour. They are a tribute from fans in Briançon.

Go into the church and you may still find yellow jerseys, team jerseys and even rainbow jerseys left in his honour. Then go to France, to the col de l'Izoard. And there, alongside a plaque to Louison Bobet, you'll find a memorial to the man who set the race alight so often.

The world has grown more sophisticated, more cynical, more educated since then. Obsessive though Italian sports fans are, it's doubtful they will ever again as much as approach the feeling that surrounded Coppi and Bartali. Italian cycling is doing well, but there have been long decades of doldrum and decay, of disinterest, of nagging belief that cycling is all big legs, poor brains and commercial corruption and self-interest.

Coppi had a magic that made all that seem unbelievable.

12 JAN JANSSEN (1940–)

I never sensed I'd have difficulty with Jan Janssen. It's funny how much you go by appearances. I remembered this open-faced chap who never looked angry but always wore sunglasses. You never saw him quoted as saying very much, but then that was probably because most cycling reporters then were French or Belgian and Janssen was one of the few Dutchmen.

The French must have felt odd about him, anyway, because he made such a point of riding in French teams. He won for them, but he also kept good honest Frenchmen out of the limelight. That is difficult to resolve in France.

He wasn't at home when I rang. His wife answered and said he'd be in Germany when I suggested calling, but he'd be back if I could leave it to the afternoon. He'd be delighted to see me. I thought my judgements about him were coming true.

I knew Putte because it was where I went for my supermarket shopping when I lived in the neighbouring village. The border runs through the middle, so south of what used to be a customs check and lorry park you'll see a mish-mash of pubs, shops and houses, and on the northern end the buildings have that eerie uniformity of Holland.

Town planning is something that came late to Belgium, but it suits both nations' characters to have things the way they are — the happy-go-lucky, haphazard Belgians and the more worrying, better organised Dutch. The last pro race of the lowland season, the Sluitingsprijs, is in the southern half. You'll see it listed as Putte–Kapellen, which is what the Belgians call it. There's no race at the Dutch end, but when they have a carnival, the funfair takes over the whole village.

I rode up through what remained of Belgium through sandy heaths and small villages as far as Kalmthout. I rode a circuit past my own house for old time's sake and noted that the current residents are better gardeners than I ever was. Then I turned down through a little place called Heide to cross into Holland. Only a change in car number-plates gives the border away.

I reached Putte alongside the Wip Er In sex cinema ('Pop In' it means, but it looks more fun in Dutch), turned right past one of the ubiquitous Albert Heijn supermarkets, and rode up through the herring stalls, *poffertje* makers (a small sweet pancake, like a Yorkshire pudding) and onto a road on the right called Postlaan. And there, several hundred yards on the left, is the factory where Jan Janssen makes bikes. He's parted with the company since my visit, but that's all that's changed since the day he won the Tour de France. He looks barely different. And until Greg LeMond's tussle with Laurent Fignon in Paris in 1989, this trim, bespectacled, blond-haired Dutchman held the record for the closest victory of all.

Jan Janssen moved to Putte at the start of 1969, from Ossendrecht further up the road. His baby Jan had just been born. Jan Janssen is the equivalent of John Smith in England or Paddy Murphy in Ireland. His house is called Mon Repos, recognising that Janssen was always the most French of the Dutch riders — Pelforth, Bic, all French.

In 1968, it was surprising that he was having lunch at Melun at all. There was nearly no Tour de France at all that year. The Americans were bombing Saigon, Martin Luther King was shot dead and President De Gaulle flew home from an interrupted tour of Romania to deal with student rioting on the streets of Paris.

Those riots, one of several around the world as young people struggled against their governments, were against the central and stifling authority of the French state, which controlled not just the radio and television stations but much else that resisted progressive thinking. Cobble stones flew and the dead and injured were transferred hourly to hospital by the dozen.

For a while it seemed all France might flare up. There were secondary riots in provincial towns in what was then this most centralised of states. And the greatest symbol outside the government of the Old Way, the traditional, the rule of the mighty against the free-thinking, was the Tour de France — 'that gaudy monument to capitalism' as the Communist *L'Humanité* called it.

Astonishingly, the riots stopped to allow the *peloton* to pass. And then they resumed.

At Melun, just before Paris, Janssen was 16 seconds back from Herman van Springel, the *maillot jaune*. He, Janssen and another Belgian, Ferdi Bracke, were all within three minutes. Just the time-trial into the capital remained; Bracke — a man capable of the world hour record — should have won. But the Grey Eminence — so called because of his prematurely lightened hair — tended to stage fright, flopping on the big occasion. Success wasn't predictable. By contrast Janssen had the calmness of Dutch tradition. A nation saved by a small boy's finger doesn't panic at a 30-mile time-trial.

Janssen was one of the last three to start. The also-rans were showered and changed in Paris and had returned in their suits or tracksuits to watch the playoff of the biggest drama the post-war Tour had known.

It took 54,600 metres to make the decision. At the end, Janssen had 54 seconds on van Springel, still more on Bracke. He had won the Tour de France. That final yellow jersey was the only one he had worn. And until LeMond, the 38 seconds which secured him victory were the smallest margin the Tour had known.

Even so, he was a winner whom Geoffrey Nicholson called among 'the more forgettable,' along with Lucien Aimar and Roger Pingeon. But Nicholson, a fair judge of men, was comparing him to Anquetil. And certainly, if the manner of his success was not crushing in the way of Anquetil or Fausto Coppi, then at least he left the race in suspense and not the foregone conclusion that so often visited it when Eddy Merckx or sometimes even Anquetil was riding.

It also began a happy sequence in which, every 21 years, the Tour put on a show. In 1947, no bookmaker would take bets on Pierre Brambilla winning, so secure were his chances on the last day. More than that, tradition demanded the *maillot jaune* was allowed his glory, undisturbed by petty attacks. But under his nose, the Breton Jean Robic — 'like a little old man in glasses with a helmet like half a dozen sausages on his head' — bobbed off on the hill out of Rouen and got enough of a lead to stand on the uppermost rostrum at the finish. Brambilla claimed afterwards to be too exhausted to follow, but it was an odd excuse for a man whose ability had dominated the race until that moment.

Twenty-one years later, it was Janssen. And then, in 1989, Greg LeMond fitted his aerodynamic tri-bars to ride through Paris for an eight-second victory over Laurent Fignon.

But for Janssen even those memories aren't enough. Nor is his rainbow jersey from 1964, won by beating Vittorio Adorni and Raymond Poulidor in a sprint at Sallanches. There is sadness in his voice. In 1969 he said: 'I shall ride another three or four years at most.' He was 29 then. 'I want to quit when I'm on top. It will never be a question of my giving up when I can no longer hang on. I know when to call it a day.'

There is sadness because that day came more quickly than he believed. Maybe he told me this because he was tired from the journey back from Germany, or maybe he just felt it anyway. But he said it all the same.

'To be honest, I had no more ambitions. It was all travelling, racing, and the results weren't so good any more. And the older you are, the more you have to prepare — train further, train more, look after yourself more, and I couldn't face all that.

'And then in '71, I was already doing a bit less — criteriums, smaller races, no Tour de France, which I found a bitter blow — and then, *ja*, I decided to give up. I was just another of the hundred or so nameless riders in the *peloton*. And then one day I was in the Tour of Luxembourg, in 1972, and I heard on the radio from one of the motorbike marshals: "Winner of the stage" ... I forget the name now ... "with the *peloton* at 15 minutes, with Jan Janssen" ... and so on and so on. And I can't tell you what a blow that was. Jan Janssen, at 15 minutes? Winner of the Tour de France, former world champion, winner of Paris–Roubaix, winner of Paris–Nice, all the big races? That couldn't be. And there and then I decided to do a couple more and then *hup*, I was done.'

We sat in the small works canteen next to the workshop. Staff came and went, among them his teenage son, who races in the black-and-white stripes of the Zuid-west Hoek ('South-west Corner') club in Bergen-op-Zoom. The three of us laughed and chatted for a moment and spoke of mutual friends. Janssen puffed on a ciga-rette, just as he did when he was racing. It's only away from the European main-land that cycling is seen as a route to health; on the Continent it has never been more than a route to money. Janssen smokes, van Est smokes, and Eddy Merckx has made a part-time living for a decade or more advertising packets of Belga.

Janssen confessed it must be difficult for his son, a young bike rider with a famous father. But while Janssen *fils* might try to overlook his father, Janssen *père* likes being recognised. Not big-headed, really, but he likes being recognised as Jan Janssen when he goes out with the keep-fit riders. He turns up on televi-sion around Tour de France time and the bike on which he rode from Melun to Paris is now part of a travelling show — he uses the English word.

I'd say he's a few pounds heavier than when he was racing. The seventies were always an odd era, with flares and tank tops and silly sunglasses and long hair and Janssen is no less embarrassed about that than anyone else. He smiles wrily at a picture of himself looking like George Best. He ticks off riders like Robert Millar and Phil Anderson with their long hair now.

I forgot for a moment that he'd ever been world champion. He never men-tioned it except in passing. I think it's the Tour rather than the championship which holds the sweetest memories. Not surprising, really.

'The Tour is the biggest race, the most beautiful race you can win,' he said. But he won it at the last moment, as an afterthought. Surely, I asked, he'd rather have won with strength, instead of taking it on the final day without having once led the journey?

'But it was much more exciting that way, wasn't it? We saw it when LeMond and Fignon decided it on the last day as well, with people crowding round the television or the radio, and the last day's a sort of climax. And it was like that for me as well.

'And I don't think I would have wanted to hold the yellow jersey longer. Right on the last day, nobody knew who would win the Tour, and that was my tactic. We had a team with three riders — Dolman, Beugels and Arie Den Hertog — and that was my team. And I was the fourth. I couldn't do anything with a team that small, could I? The other riders had packed up and gone home.

'So what could I do? I had to be very smart to win the Tour and the only chance was to do it in the time-trial.'

Two decades have passed, but those sensations that LeMond and Fignon must have known are still fresh to him. It took Janssen only a second to remember the gap between Bracke, van Springel and himself, and none at all to recall the number of seconds that put him in yellow.

It's a back-to-front distinction, to win the world's biggest race with the smallest ever margin. And now he can't even boast that.

'Records are made to be broken,' he said. '*Ja.*' He puffed again and stubbed out the remains.

'I was in Paris for LeMond and Fignon. I stood along the Champs Elysées. That's not where we finished, of course, but it brought back wonderful memories for me, that Tour de France. It has changed technically over the years, but the Tour is still the greatest sporting event in the world, and if you can manage to win it, then you've achieved the most beautiful thing that the sport has to offer.'

It was the last year the Tour was public property. For the next four years it went to Eddy Merckx and the sport moved from a number of big-hitters to just one.

I suggested that the game in Janssen's era was more exciting. Not to my surprise, he agreed.

'I'll go along with that. In my time, a lot of riders could have won. In the time of Merckx, Hinault, Coppi, it was a lot more predictable. You knew in advance who was going to win. Merckx was in the yellow jersey from the second day and the others couldn't touch him. And for the public, the people who follow the sport on television and radio, that was less spectacular.

'When I rode the Tour, there were 10, 15 good riders. First one would win and then the next and then the next. But in the Merckx era, the Hinault era, all the races were the same. So the public got fed up.

'Now, of course, there aren't any big names such as Merckx. You've got very good riders, but …'

'Nobody like Jan Janssen?' I prompted.

'Who am I to say that?'

And then, as his son left to busy himself around the warehouse, I asked Janssen whether he had been born too soon, whether he would rather be his son's age.

'It's certainly changed now, that's for sure. It's more commercial, and the generation before me, Wim van Est's generation, they say it as well — we were born too early. There's much more money to be earned.'

And that made it easier for him?

'Not easier. We had to be good all the time, from the first of February until the end of October. Because it was my duty to make the most of my sponsor's name, to get publicity. I mean, there were other good riders in the team, but it was 80 per cent on my shoulders to get that publicity. And if you had an off-day, well, you were letting your sponsors down.'

So why, I wanted to know, is there more money now if in his own estimation the races aren't so exciting?

'Because the whole sponsorship of sport has taken off. It's become so interesting to a company because a company that wants to get its name known, you can buy a good team, with good management, good public relations, and you can get all the big names.

'But it didn't use to be like that, because the television in our time … well, it was covered but not like now. Direct coverage for an hour and a half they have. Naturally, that is very interesting for the public.

'We got very good money, of course. And to be truthful, the French franc was worth a lot more than now. But I think the motivation has changed with the professionals as well. You get riders like Rooks and Theunisse saying after the Tour they are stopping at home because they can't be bothered with criteriums, and that's not attractive to the public. I don't think you're serving the sport doing that, because the more popular cycling is, the better it is for every one of the riders.'

In Janssen's day, riders didn't grow rich from the Tour. They rode for publicity and made their money from criterium engagements that followed. Now it's the other way round.

'It's good that they're well paid now, of course, but they have to give everything they've got. And now there are a load of riders who say "I only want to ride the classics in the spring and no Tour de France, no Giro d'Italia and no Tour of Spain, because it's too hot there and there are too many mountains, and there's this and there's that."

'And there are riders who say they're not going to ride Paris–Roubaix over the bad roads, and no Tour of Flanders in the snow and rain. They pick and choose their races.

'Well, it didn't use to be that way. You got a list of races from your team manager and you had to ride them.

'You can't have a new Merckx or Hinault every couple of years, because people like that are rare, but what I would say is that the general level of top riders has gone down a bit. There are a number of good riders but no big-hitters any more. The whole sport has changed. They aren't hungry any more. There's so much money to earn now, even for a third-rate rider. Twenty-five years ago, a third-class rider did not get jam on his bread. So if they got 50 guilders for a criterium, they rode. But now every rider is well paid, but they don't do so much for it. They say "Oh, I've got a good contract from the firm, I'm okay."

'The hunger to ride well, to succeed and only then to earn money is over.'

He's not bitter, I sense. Despairing perhaps, but realistic would be a better word. In 1967, by the way, Janssen nearly won the world championship for a second time. But he was, in two ways, just that little too late. To start with, he was half a wheel too late. But mainly, he had left it too late to try, because he was now a mature man and with him was a youthful Eddy Merckx — just three years after the Belgian had won the world amateur race.

On the second lap at Heerlen, where Graham Webb and Beryl Burton had already won, there was an attack by Gianni Motta. So Merckx, the Spaniard Saez, and Holland's van der Vleuten went with him. Merckx wrote later: 'There was also an unknown Briton called Addy, who never took his turn and disappeared quickly.'

Bob Addy was a tall home-based professional in the Holdsworth domestic team, who now runs a bike shop in Watford, Hertfordshire. How easily are one man's dream moments dispelled!

Motta had been given excruciating distances to ride in training by a guru, half-doctor, half-svengali, and he was at that stage where fitness risked toppling into exhaustion. Eventually Dr De Donato would attract the attentions of the police, but for the moment he had Motta in peak condition.

How confident he felt you can judge by the fact there were still 250km to go. The bunch wondered at his foolhardiness for a while; then, after the break had gained three minutes in 60 kilometres, began wondering again. There was a flurry of concern and the motorcycle blackboard man brought the break the news that Janssen had decided to chase.

That was bad news. Janssen was a brilliant sprinter — he beat Merckx on the line in Ghent–Wevelgem — and, what's more, he'd proved in the Tour de France that he had the time-trialling ability to close a three-minute gap.

Motta turned to the blackboard again and saw the numbers of the break, then a horizontal line with Janssen's number below it. And below Janssen, a large oval to indicate the bunch.

'Who's with him?' Motta shouted. There were numbers missing, surely?

'Nobody,' the motorcyclist yelled back. 'He's by himself.'

The Italian turned to Merckx and called on him in broken French to work with him in staying away. Merckx wrote later in *Eddy Merckx, Coureur Cycliste* that Janssen was one of the few he considered a 'true athlete.' But he wasn't going to work to stop him.

Instead, he calculated that Janssen would be weakened by the chase but still strong enough to work to keep the group clear. More than that, the Dutch team — usually better organised than the Belgians, whom nobody could guarantee wouldn't chase Merckx for their own purposes — would ease off if Janssen stood a chance. So too might anyone in Janssen's team grateful for a contract for the following year. What's more, van der Vleuten was already in the break.

In fact Peter Post did chase, but then equally Janssen did work with van der Vleuten. The Dutch figured that they alone had two in the break.

Before winning the amateur championship, Merckx told his mother in Brussels that he would shake his legs on a downhill stretch to indicate he felt fresh in the closing miles. He shook his legs and Mrs Merckx was delighted. Young Eddy said later he had done it because they were tired.

This time he remembered the wigging he got. As the bell rang for the last 13km lap, he winked into the television camera. It was the message to the folk back home.

But afterwards he admitted: 'It looked confident, but frankly I wasn't that certain.'

Motta jumped on the last descent but failed. Janssen waited for the last 100 metres to sprint and Merckx leaped first. Through his arms, Merckx could see the Dutchman coming up on him inch by inch. Five metres before the line, he was alongside. Desperately, Merckx flung his bike forward beneath him and won by half a wheel.

Jan Janssen had to face his home crowd disappointed.

13 BERYL BURTON (1937–)

On the weekend that Jan Janssen missed the world championship, Britain scored more road medals in a day than ever in history.

In the 100-mile championship that year of 1967, when Beryl Burton won the women's road race, she was followed for a few miles by a police car — one of those big white ones with the orange and blue stripes. She probably grew irritated at the thought that it was another well-meaning but misguided spectator, since it is not in the nature of police cars to follow champion racing cyclists, and she would have worried about disqualification.

After a while the steady purr of the engine hardened and the car moved nearer. As it swung out to pass, its loudhailer bellowed: 'Come on, Beryl, keep it up.'

Beryl Burton had that sort of appeal, at the same time mumsy and exceptional, that meant even non-cyclists knew her, just as they had heard of but would never have recognised Reg Harris. Added to which, she worked on a rhubarb farm, which made her more loveable yet.

You'd never say she looked like an athlete. An athlete's mum, perhaps, but not the athlete herself. She's never had the waifness of runners and jumpers. Her friends would never call her elfin. She's not even big and butch. The thing you notice is that she looks so very unremarkable. We shared accommodation in Tucson, Arizona, once and I remember not tales of heroics or 'my favourite races' but idle chatter about her wish to throw open every window in her home and why it should be that modern kitchens never have enough power points.

We were there — she as a guest, because she'd been hurt in a traffic crash — for a three-day international. The Americans treated her with awe and respect. She never seemed to notice it, still less seek it. She simply enjoyed the sunshine on her bike, returning browner each day to remark how slowly Americans drove.

'It's all like a dream-land,' she said.

And yet in a race, she was transformed: locked in place, her saddle a little low, one hand higher than the other.

In 30 years she won seven world championship gold medals (five pursuits and two road races), three silver and four bronze; twelve golds and two silvers for the national road race; twenty-five consecutive BBAR titles at time-trialling; 72 national championship and 50 competition records from 10 miles to 12 hours; thirteen gold pursuit championship medals, one silver and one bronze; and two pursuit records.

Her hundred-plus championships are more than four times better than the men's best of 25 by Ian Hallam, between 1969 and 1982. That isn't simply because there are fewer women than men. If all her best rides had been in 1974, she would have won the *men's* BBAR.

She wasn't the first woman to dominate. As she joined Morley Cycling Club, near Leeds, the woman of the day was Eileen Sheridan. She lives now in a pretty house on the bank of the Thames in London.

Sheridan looked too dainty to ride a bike. She had curly hair and minute black shorts. And yet she rode 237 miles in a 12 in 1949, won the BBAR in 1949 and 1950, and then turned professional for Hercules. Her records included 446 miles for a straight-out 24 hours and, in 1954, Land's End–John o'Groats in two days, eleven hours and seven minutes. Beryl Burton had a lot to follow.

In 1967, British cycling was down in the dumps after Tom Simpson's death. The men's track team at the world championships was pulling itself to bits with personality problems, there was no natural hope for the professionals, and the rider likely to do best in the amateur road squad, Graham Webb, was the very man some accused of being gormless.

Burton, by her standards, failed in the track championships and lost her gold in the pursuit. She came to Limburg, in that bit of Holland where Belgium and Germany all come nestling in, in a foul mood. The team manager was an abrasive, chinny Londoner called Chas Messenger, who'd made himself a dubious celebrity during his time as Tour of Britain organiser by taking the route over more hills than any man might decently wish.

And now, from his counterpart in the track team, he had inherited Burton.

She sat in the team hotel, complaining: 'I've failed; there's only one medal that matters.'

Messenger recalled: 'Beryl came with a chip on her shoulder a yard wide, and it wouldn't have taken much for her to have sloshed me. Beryl and I are old sparring partners, and eventually I reminded her that we had, in fact, never had a real stand-up fight, and the ruffled feathers began to calm down.' Messenger's nerves were already taut. The night before the championships started, he had heard in his hotel room that he'd been sacked, replaced as manager of the Olympic team.

He and masseur Eddie Soens, a Liverpudlian with a reputation for developing latent talent in riders, put the will to win back in her again. And then Messenger went off to reflect on his own miseries, having sorted out the other road riders as well.

'Here I had the team of teams, the cream that comes but once to a manager's coffee ... for what? To go back and be tossed aside at the whim of who knows who?' he said. The British Cycling Federation never commented publicly on why it had done it.

Messenger put bottles of champagne on ice at the hotel before the women's and the men's championship. Both obliged. Graham Webb won the men's race alone, and Burton did the same with the women.

Alan Gayfer, reporting for *Cycling*, said of Burton: 'One had the impression that, had she gone on, she would have started to lap some of the field — and the figures confirmed this, for a Swiss, an Austrian and a West German finished 17 minutes behind her and she was taking 21 minutes a lap. They had lost the 17 minutes in three laps.'

It is difficult to make exciting reporting of a race in which one rider goes away from the start and stays there. It is difficult to make a heroine of someone who says afterwards that it wasn't much of a race anyway. But these things you have to live with.

Burton was on the front of the starting grid as she waited with 42 others. The distance was 33 miles, short compared with the men but fast as a result, and hilly for Holland. The flag dropped, they all rode five miles together, and then Burton tried riding away from them all. Never did she have an attacking sprint; she went in the way she'd always won before, by stretching them out until they broke. The little bunch strung out for 100 yards, frayed at the back as the weaker ones vanished to international ignominy after just six miles, and then there were just two jerseys — one blue and one red.

Burton, in blue, ended the lap with a look as black as she'd had in the hotel. The Russian was permanently on her wheel. She was an unknown from a nation which dependably provided real risks.

Again Burton had no sudden switch and jump to displace her. So she waited for the Ubachsberg hill, rolled up it ever faster, and then switched into her 104-inch top and pressed down the other side.

Zadorozhnaya said she feared to keep up, terrified for her leg muscles. Burton had her own fears.

'I got cramps towards the end and thought "Oh no, I'm not going to finish up like Les West [who had a name for cramping up at vital moments] and lose everything." I didn't think I was really fit enough to be able to stay away like that, but I just put the pressure on all the time. No one told me how far ahead I was or whether I was gaining or not, so I just kept going.'

The Russian wasn't rubbish, either. Alone, just like Burton, she nevertheless kept the rest of the world's best at four minutes, including the up-and-coming domestic hope, Keetie Hage. At the same time, Burton could take her for 'only' 1-47.

The new world champion — the oldest women's champion there'd been — looked hardly ruffled.

'I've ridden harder races and finished more shattered,' she said.

In the unkind way of these things, the men attracted more attention than the women. And Graham Webb, an outsider to all except those who had seen him lap criterium fields in Holland that season, appeared to be on the edge of a pro career as he pulled on the first rainbow jersey a British amateur roadman had won since lord knows when.

But Burton's real talent showed not in Holland that day but a few weeks later, in September, on 277 miles of road around York and Boroughbridge. Then, in the Otley CC 12-hour, she beat not simply the women's record but rode faster than any man in history. The result: Beryl Burton 277.2 miles, Mike McNamara, a men's record of 276.8.

It's difficult not to feel sorry for McNamara.

Forbidden to place men and women in the same race, the organisers had followed the convention of running one event immediately after the other. Tradition has it that the fastest are separated by ten minutes, to prevent what are intended to be solo rides ending up as road races. But Burton and McNamara were in different races, and therefore nothing prevented Mac being seeded last to start among the men, number 129, and Burton being the first woman off (number 131) two minutes later. The gap in the numbering marks the token extra minute used to 'separate' the men from the women.

Both saw the significance the moment the start order dropped through their letter boxes a week before the race. Burton claims she had no intention of riding just to catch McNamara, that she was 'just out to have a good ride round.' But it's easier to believe that a woman who took it into her mind to crush the best road riders in the world didn't have at least a twinkling ambition to catch McNamara.

Certainly her preparations suggested more than a casual air.

'You should have seen it at our house the night before,' she said. 'We had food all lined up on the breakfast bar. There was fruit salad, peaches, rice pudding, fruit and honey cake, egg and milk, peppermint and blackcurrant, coffee, glucose, malt bread, bananas, four bits of steak and some cheese.

'Nim Carline [a clubmate and distance champion] came in, looked at all this and said: "What on earth do you want all that for in a 12?" I said I intended to go out for a day's ride to enjoy myself.'

Casual, eh? Yet she was aware of the pressure on McNamara when she got to the start, knowing he had already said he wanted to set a record time to be sure of the BBAR, knowing too that he had a world champion 120 seconds behind him.

'I got to the start just before Mac went off, and I felt sorry for him. I knew he was chasing the record and I was glad I wasn't on his saddle, chasing 275 miles.'

She went for a three-mile warm-up, then kicked herself at the stupidity of it. There would be more than enough time to loosen up in 12 hours.

To Tadcaster, to York and then to Thirsk and back, first one and then the other had the advantage. At 100 miles Mac led by 57 seconds.

Burton said: 'I didn't really think I would finish. I thought if I lasted four hours I would be all right, but at the back of my mind I thought I would pack it in before the finish. Several times I had Mac in sight, but it never occurred to me to go after him.

'I even stopped at 4fi hours to have a bottle of water on my head and to go to the other side of the hedge, which was where I nearly lost a minute on him.'

Then she got stomach-ache and went through that kitchen-table inventory — ginger beer, peppermint, blackcurrant, anything that might help. She was in distress until her husband Charly (the spelling honours the little Luxembourgeois climber Charly Gaul) found a small bottle of brandy and handed it over 'for medicinal purposes only, Beryl.'

It took another 100 miles to make up what she had lost. She passed 200 miles in 8-33-37 and Mac passed in 8-33-55. Only two more riders were inside nine hours.

The only other bad patch was more mechanical than medical. She was alone on the road when an oscillation set up under her saddle. It was minute, but it repeated with each turn of the wheels, and her wheels were turning steadily at 24mph.

When you're alone, it's a feeling worse than a puncture — the sensation of a wheel that might be about to collapse. A puncture can be mended with a spare tyre; a broken wheel needs a workshop.

'The noise and the wobbling drove me wild and I couldn't see Charly any-where.' One broken spoke could produce more within moments. The ride of rides could end with her head in her hands on the grass verge. Charly was in the car, keen not to be seen too close to her because of the rule that said he couldn't be. It had never happened to Beryl — something to do with her general popularity, perhaps, even among those whom she regularly beat — but there had been rumours for years that certain officials were out to 'get' riders whose helpers kept tightly up behind them.

'When he did come up, I was really cross. I could foresee my wheel collapsing and me missing valuable time sitting by the side of the road. I said "That'll teach you to follow a bit closer. Everyone else has cars following them quite close so they can see when something goes wrong, why can't you follow closely?" Of course, I apologised to him afterwards, and Charly said I went like a rocket when the new wheel was put in, even though I had lost very little time at all.'

The funny side is that, while Beryl is not especially big, Charly is decidedly little. He is 5ft 6in and 8fi stone. Together, they look like a seaside cartoon by Donald McGill. Both see the joke. After the Sportswriters' Association dinner, Beryl said: 'He has decided to let me off for kissing Henry Cooper the other week.'

It was at the dinner, where she won the sportswoman of the year award alongside the motorcyclist Mike Hailwood, that she made her most public recognition of the part 'the lad' had taken in her successes.

'On the Continent,' she said, 'it requires a flotilla of helpers to keep a rider at the top — sponsors, manager, mechanic, *soigneur*, masseur, *domestique* — whereas I've got my hubby; in fact it has become quite a giggle at some events now, because if I win or do a record time, some of the lads go and congratulate Charly!'

Long-distance time-trials finish on circuits of 10 to 20 miles. Timekeepers sit on folding stools at mile intervals and log each rider past. Calculations show where, between each timing point, a rider would have been when time finally ran out. The idea is to prevent the high and the lowly being separated by several counties — not entirely an impossibility — and all the timekeeping and measuring problems that would cause.

Burton and Mac were only seconds apart as they entered the 16-mile Otley circuit at 206 miles. But the psychological effect of those final laps differed. Burton started to close up.

'It was so strange, really, because though I knew I was on a record, it didn't impress me. Normally I would go a bit berserk chasing a record, but it didn't mean anything to me.' On the second circuit she caught him at 235 miles.

'Would you like a liquorice?' she asked him.

'Ta, love,' said McNamara, and Burton cruised by. McNamara ate the liquorice. Some, including the cartoonist Johnny Helms, thought it might better have been kept as a little bit of history.

McNamara had been pushed to 276.52 miles, nearly five miles better than Owen Blower's record, good enough to secure him the BBAR; she, unbelievably, rode 277.25, twenty-seven better than ever before. At 7.11 that evening, just less than two minutes after McNamara had finished, Burton pulled up alongside timekeeper Arnold Elsegood with 45 seconds still to go,

'I didn't fancy another ride up that hill,' she told him as she reached for her water bottle and waited for Charly. The women's record had passed the men's for the first and only time in history.

She wasn't sure whether she regarded it as her greatest ride. She just wanted to go home. At 9pm she was in bed, at 1.30am she was up again to clean the car of all the 12-hour detritus, 'so that the lad wouldn't have too much to do when he got up.' And at 3am they set off for the London six-day race and cycle show, where she was received as a hero. Next morning, after getting back to bed at 3.30am, she went training. In the autumn she went cycling in Portugal, wondering whether an outbreak of foot-and-mouth on farms in the Lake District would stop her spending Christmas on her bike there.

Burton and McNamara met again at the Road Time Trials Council's champions night, where they received their BBAR trophies.

'I've right let meself down,' he confessed, to which the audience bellowed 'No, no.'

He had, in the BBAR and his record, fulfilled his life's ambition. But perhaps, Alan Gayfer reflected afterwards, he would never live down the fact that Burton beat him in his finest hour.

14 FEDERICO BAHAMONTES (1929–)

There are, said Jan Janssen, no great stars as there were in his day. There are also, incidentally, no hotels in Putte. The carnival crowd were still going full tilt in the village. But dusk was falling and I wanted to get away. It was out of my way, but the best bet seemed to be to ride north to Bergen-op-Zoom.

The Dutch are almost scared of the dark. They ride huge black roadster bikes that went out of fashion here along with district nurses and cycling parsons; and every one of those Gazelles and Batavus has both reflectors threaded between the spokes and dynamos to light the way home. But they're off the road at night as soon as they can.

They ride home to tiny houses with minute gardens in roads named after mayors, priests and local artists. And there they spend their evenings in rooms brightly lit and uncurtained to passers-by. Drawing the curtains suggests to the Dutch that there is something to hide. A hint of pretence or scandal. The old ways are changing, and the neighbours doubtless talk about the trendsetters, but for the moment Holland hides its secrets not by curtains but by improbable quantities of window plants.

It was the same in Bergen-op-Zoom as elsewhere. The name, like so many in Holland, is a joke. The Dutch acquired surnames at the insistence of the invading French, and took their revenge by choosing names that Napoléon wouldn't understand. The French would go home before long, they reasoned, and they could get back to life as it had been before.

Sadly, the habit stuck and you'll still meet people with names like High Bosom, Pancake and, distressingly, Shit-on-the-Doorstep. The Dutch have made it worse for themselves with a law that makes a new name forbiddingly difficult to adopt.

Anyway, Bergen-op-Zoom means Hills-on-the-Edge. The second part is true enough, since the sea's not far away, but you can only surmise that those who thought there were hills there had never seen the Alps.

I was reflecting on that and the 'real' hills of southern Europe when I recalled one of those stars of the Janssen era who's long since vanished.

There's a story that everyone will tell you about Federico Martin Alejandra Bahamontes. It's of the day he rode in his funny upright style, back straight, hands grasping the straights of his bars, to the top of an Alpine pass.

Those were days when climbers routinely opened large gaps on the strugglers below, but this lead was remarkable in itself. And there, at the peak, Bahamontes stopped, cadged a pistachio ice-cream — his favourite — and sat on a low stone wall waiting for the rest to arrive. It was the first time he had done it in the Tour de France, but the Spanish journalists were expecting it. It was a repeat of what he'd done elsewhere, the action of a man content to win in the mountains but accepting that he'd rarely win a stage race overall.

He did eventually gather his nerves about descending the mountains alone. But for the moment he thought of the unguarded bends and of men like Roger Rivière and Wim van Est, both of whom had disastrously missed their footing and plunged terrifyingly into the depths. Bahamontes was brave on his bike but timid by nature, and, so it's said, never forgot the pain and ignominy of careering into a cactus bush while descending the Montserra as an amateur.

Rivals dismissed him as a fool. He already puzzled them enough by his habit of talking about himself in the third person — 'Federico was tired today, but tomorrow he will attack again,' he'd say. And he was unpredictable.

He'd had enough on the col de Luitel in the Tour de France of 1956 and slung his bike into a ravine rather than let his manager persuade him to continue. In 1957, his team-mates waving their fists and his manager Luis Puig arguing with him volubly, Bahamontes simply tugged off his shoes and climbed into the sag wagon. Miguel Poblet had already left the race and, without his support, that was enough.

'But you are a giant, you can do it without Poblet,' Puig argued.

'No.'

'But Federico, you must. For your mother, for your dear mother.'

Bahamontes shook his head.

'Please Federico — for your mother.'

'No.'

'For Spain, for beloved Spain, then?'

'No.'

'For Franco.'

'*No, no, no!*'

Bahamontes threw his shoes into the *voiture balai* and climbed in after them.

He was nothing unless there were hills. He rarely left Spain and never succeeded except in the mountains. A charming picture shows him boarding a train after just three days of the 1960 Tour de France, eliminated on a stage with no more than a pimple to its name.

When he was good, he was brilliant. But sometimes he could be belittled. The 1957 Tour of Spain was one of those times.

Bahamontes had a dreadful rival in Spain, a man from the Basque country called Jesus Lorono. Where one went the other followed, like the crocodile and Captain Hook. Within two days it was a feud. And where stars fall out, others are liable to gain.

Raphaël Géminiani was the man. On the fourth stage he broke away with eight others. It was appalling weather even for mountain Spain, and the snow built up as the race wore on. Before long it proved impossible to reach the finish on top of the col de Pajares, and the organisers drove through the race shouting that it would finish in five miles' time.

By then the leaders had two minutes, and within the five miles they had doubled it. Bahamontes was race leader but still ignored the challenge to keep on taunting Lorono. Behind them, riders were finishing as much as two hours down, forcing the organisers to cancel the stage as riders huddled around log fires and their clothing steamed.

Bahamontes soon paid the price. On the road from Valencia to Torosa, Lorono slipped into a break that ran up a 22-minute lead. Bahamontes was finished.

The journalists, of course, were bitter. All promise and no punch, they said. And they were right, because in 1958, the following year, he cracked beneath an attack by little Charly Gaul, the fleck-mouthed rider from Luxembourg.

But suddenly the boy who promised much and delivered little — leaving aside his national championship and the fact that he'd been king of the mountains in the Tour de France of 1954, of course, which journalists are prone to do — this boy with the promise that stayed stubbornly hidden came good.

He took on Gaul on stage 10 of the Tour and together they whipped their chasers into a 14-minute defeat across the Pyrénées. When Gaul cracked in the Massif Central, Bahamontes' win in the Tour de France took him back to Spain a national hero, received by General Franco.

It wasn't a satisfying encounter.

Bahamontes recalled: 'I went to see him at Pardo and he questioned me about tennis and football, but I couldn't really help him because he supported Real Madrid and I was a Barcelona supporter. At the end of our interview, he thanked me for what I'd done for the country.'

They always called him the Eagle of Toledo, but it was a false name. Eagle, yes, but Toledo scarcely. Bahamontes' family background is Cuban rather than Spanish, and Federico was only a child when his father Julian took him from Toledo to Madrid to escape the civil war in Castilia.

Years later he recalled: 'My father was neither a red nor a fascist. He just didn't like the idea of people coming along and demanding he give away the olives, butter and chickens into which he had put so much work. So we left Toledo.'

Even so, the town held a party for him, celebrating at the gates of the market where the young Spaniard had loaded and unloaded fruit crates for pocket money.

Bahamontes was like a firework sparkler. He was difficult to light, brilliant at his peak, but went out quickly. He swung from gaiety to spectacular depression, from which he could be lifted by some tiny gift, like a square of chocolate.

In the Margnat team, Raoul Rémy said of him: 'He never had a strategy in the mountains. He just didn't want anyone on his wheel.' Bahamontes himself — who wandered the streets at night after Tour stages and didn't stumble on the benefits of massage or a controlled diet until well into his career — said: 'I always did best on the really hot days because then my opponents couldn't take as much dope as they would have liked. But I didn't use the stuff myself because I was always too nervous.'

He was six times the best climber of the Tour in just 10 years, in a career that started against Fausto Coppi and ended alongside Jacques Anquetil.

Like so many, he failed to shake off the Frenchman as he reached his peak. In 1964, at 35, he finished second to Anquetil and a year later third to Anquetil and Raymond Poulidor.

But like that sparkler, he faded rapidly. He was diminished to blackness in the very Pyrénées he once governed; on the stage from Bagnères-de-Bigorre he scraped inside the time limit, 40 minutes back on Julio Jimenez, another Spaniard.

Next day Bahamontes made a foolish attack on the banks of the Garonne, got partway up the col du Portet d'Aspet, swung his leg over the saddle, and waited for the bus to collect him.

15 RAYMOND POULIDOR (1936–)

Poulidor is black-haired with a deep tan. He says little and smiles slowly. Once, at a world championship, I walked alongside the fence and sensed what it must be to be him — a wave of cheers arose as the crowd spotted the man behind me.

'*Pou-pou, pou-pou*,' they shouted. Their eyes were alight, their faces a picture of delight. He must get that wherever he goes. I wonder whether he tires of it.

He must hate being called *pou-pou*. It isn't simply friendly, a contraction of the word for 'doll.' It also means doll-brain.

Poulidor's another of those stars that Jan Janssen hinted at. Teams work now for their main chance; they have leaders but they don't have Leaders. A cartoon in *Cycling* once pictured a pro team as a brawny sprinter, a spindly, nervous climber, several *domestiques* with their foreheads low and their eyes suspiciously close together — and Le Leader. He is gazing into his reflection. Small arrows point to Les Legs Bronze, a yellow jersey labelled Le Perfect Fit, and a halo.

Admittedly Poulidor never had that. Jock Wadley once found him hoeing a field in a Mercier tracksuit.

But he is in all the pictures that typify the Tour of the 1960s. In one, the col de l'Iseran in 1963, Poulidor, Anquetil and Bahamontes are locked together on the road to Chamonix. The other is of the Puy-de-Dôme on July 12, 1964.

The Puy is an old volcano, a freak hill near Clermont-Ferrand. The Tour organisers reckon there are half a million people between the bottom and the top.

To put this climb of 1964 into perspective, you have to go back a few days. You have to go back to the stage after the rest day in Andorra, the mountain state then administered alternately by France and Spain.

The bunch had made its way south through France with nothing yet to set it on fire. The yellow jersey had moved from Rudi Altig, the crewcut German, to his physical opposite, the pixie-like Georges Groussard. Journalists amused themselves in the absence of anything better with a prediction that Anquetil would abandon the race after 13 stages. There was no more validity to Magician Belline's words than any other crackpot fortune-teller's, but it was good fun and it amused the superstitious.

Oddly, Anquetil did feel ill in Andorra. Spanish food didn't agree with him, and word, of course, flew round the town. Antonin Magne walked straight to Poulidor's room and told him to attack in the morning. Poulidor nodded in agreement.

In fact it was Bahamontes who went first and Poulidor moved up to him. Anquetil was left standing, his face distorted. The magician, by contrast, was smiling. Anxious now, Anquetil's team fluttered round him like birds around an injured starling. They tried to draw him out of the bunch, pushing him on the climb despite the protests of organiser Jacques Goddet. But disaster rode with every turn of Poulidor's Campagnolo pedals.

By the summit of the first ascent, Poulidor was leading the Tour de France. He had four minutes, more than Anquetil could hope to win back. Yet the misery of the climb had enervated the Norman. The stress was out of his legs as the road flattened briefly at the summit.

He grabbed a newspaper from a spectator, took his hands off the curved handlebar tops to poke it under his yellow jersey, and embarked on the descent.

This was no summer's day. The sky was black, just as it was when Merckx led Ocana on his devil's ride, and although there was no rain, an icy blast buffeted its way around the hairpins. Nobody knows how many times Anquetil nearly fell in his pursuit of Poulidor. Nobody knows because nobody could stay with him.

Fourteen miles from the mountain-top, he caught the chasing group of Groussard, Foucher, Monty and Anglade. Together, deep in the Ariège valley, they reached Poulidor and Bahamontes. Anquetil was back now as leader both overall and on the road, but he was weak. And Poulidor, although psychologically bruised by having his hopes snatched, hadn't just been chasing for 20 miles or more.

And then, extraordinarily, two things happened which typify Poulidor's luck. First he punctured. And then, as his mechanic pushed, he fell off. In more gentlemanly days, riders preferred not to profit from rivals' mishaps. But chivalry is long dead and Anquetil was off down the road. Attack was also to the benefit of Groussard's Pelforth-Sauvage team, and they went as well.

From leading at lunchtime, Poulidor was two minutes behind Anquetil at Toulouse and four and a quarter minutes adrift of Groussard's yellow jersey. Worse, he was 2:52 behind Anquetil overall and in sixth place.

And that, with minor changes, was how it stayed until Anquetil used the time-trial from Peyrehorade to Bayonne to displace Groussard. Five days passed then. The Alps were a memory and the target was the Puy. Poulidor had cut his deficit to 57 seconds.

The road across the Puy winds and twists doggedly. These days it's the venue for all the Dutch spectators. Coach companies from all over Holland run trips specifically to Puy-de-Dôme and there's more Dutch spoken on its slopes than French. Then, though, there were many more French, with other nationalities also there through the pioneering Eurovision broadcasts.

The photographs show just Anquetil and Poulidor. It is irrelevant that Julio Jimenez is so far ahead that he could never be caught. Anquetil is salt-crusted, his yellow jersey stained from sweat. Poulidor is in purple and yellow, the word Mercier (the bike, not the champagne company) on his chest and the initials BP on his short yellow sleeves. He is wearing a hat, Anquetil is bare-headed. They are side by side, Anquetil crouched low with his toes pointing down, Poulidor sitting more conventionally.

More than once, they are so close that they bang shoulders.

Those who know about long climbs say the secret is not in speed, although that's important. It's in rhythm. Drummers call it a groove — the ability to lock into evenly repeated actions that carry you smoothly and safely ahead. Both Anquetil and Poulidor realised it. They rode alongside each other, each trying to impose his rhythm, his average speed, on the other. And neither would surrender.

Several times Poulidor tested him and several times more Anquetil retaliated. They wriggled and writhed upwards, the world's two best climbers ahead of them, the struggling mass out of sight below.

Nobody's sure where Anquetil cracked. Some say it was a couple of kilometres from the summit. Others say it was less than 500 metres. And some say Anquetil merely eased, knowing Poulidor couldn't get enough to beat him in the time-trial. There was no weaving, little sign of distress. Poulidor just bobbed ahead and Anquetil rode after him, first by a little, then by 42 seconds.

By the summit, Anquetil was leader by merely 14 seconds. That much more and Poulidor would have worn the yellow jersey for the only time in his life. But the race was still in the south, a long way from Paris. There were calculations the length of Europe to decide how well Anquetil would win the closing time-trial, from Versailles to the Parc des Princes in Paris. That he *would* win was inevitable; the question was how much Poulidor could make up between the Puy and Versailles. If that was 14 seconds plus the difference in the time-trial, Poulidor would win. If not …

It never happened. There was nothing that Poulidor could do that Anquetil could not master. Anquetil won the time-trial and Poulidor was second overall by 55 seconds.

There had never been a greater show on earth.

Anquetil, of course, is no longer with us. Poulidor lives still where he has always lived, at La Creuse, in Limousin. He spends the summers in a home on the coast that he won during the Tour de France. He probably plays cards with friends. He's a formidable poker player, something that taciturn face and deep eyes do nothing to hinder. He was well aware of how his natural shyness, as the French took it to be, benefited his cause, and he played on it. He's nobody's fool.

He's also no pauper. Legend always tells of Anquetil's quarry and bike factory and other investments, because Anquetil was always painted the city slicker. But winning the Tour of Spain (1964), Paris–Nice (1972 and 1973), Milan–San Remo (1961) and coming thrice second and five times third in the Tour de France leaves nobody unpaid.

It still amuses him that he and Anquetil were built up as enemies. French television has a set list of heroes — the singer Johnny Halliday, a handful of others, and Raymond Poulidor. I saw him talking once, slowly and clearly and with some amusement, about those days. He was never famous for anything other than riding a bike. He's only well known now because he *used* to ride a bike and because he used to keep coming second. Odd, really.

The truth is that Poulidor and Anquetil rarely spoke. But then Poulidor rarely spoke much to anyone anyway, and Anquetil had a justifiable reputation for aloofness. They would neither of them have been great company on a long train journey. More than once Poulidor denied any coolness, even less any hatred, but by then it was in nobody's interest to believe him. France was having too much fun. All you can say is that they never rode in the same trade team and that both ended up better off for it.

Anquetil, more guardedly, said: 'Of course I would like to see Poulidor win the Tour de France — in my absence.' The closing condition was no more than anybody might have said — why would he have wished defeat on himself? — but what was at worst only a mischievous gesture was interpreted as more. Anquetil encouraged this when he added: 'I have beaten him so often that his victory would only add to my reputation.'

He also repeated that it was van Looy, not Poulidor, who frightened him. And that, too, was seen as a snub, because van Looy was no climber. But then again, the Belgian was as crafty as Anquetil and he respected him for that.

Anquetil was as clever with his words as Harold Wilson, and in Raymond Poulidor he had his Edward Heath.

Not that Poulidor couldn't lard his own words. When one year he fell off after a crash with a motorcycle photographer and had to leave the race at Albi, he announced with what you can take either as grandness or self-deprecation: 'The Tour de France will continue even in my absence.'

There were shades in the Anquetil–Poulidor rivalry of the differences between Coppi and Bartali a decade and a half earlier. Poulidor was the country-man's favourite, and they pointed to Anquetil's persistent use and campaigning for drugs as evidence of their own man's purity. And, assuredly, Poulidor never failed a dope test. But nor was he impartial on the issue of drug tests.

In 1967, the year that Tom Simpson died during the Tour de France, Poulidor was among those — including world champion Rudi Altig — who refused to take a test.

In 1966, two of the new drug-test doctors walked into Poulidor's hotel room and demanded a urine sample there and then. The conclusion is that they had chosen a big name rather than pick off some lesser-light who would disappear and never be heard of again.

Poulidor agreed, it is said, with reluctance. No more was heard of the test, but within an hour the news was across town. Next day the bunch started the stage, then climbed off and walked. The Tour organisers had received a message about the wisdom of future tests.

The Tour de France, though, has never been a humble organisation and it sought a showdown with the troublemakers. If it couldn't get them directly, it would punish them through their sponsors. Next year's Tour would be for national teams and they would have to put up with it. Ironically, it was the decision which gave Simpson the freedom to attempt victory and which, in the end, led to his death from drugs. And it was his death which brought the modern era of testing that the riders had been trying to avoid.

But on balance, Poulidor was a man who brought fun to the Tour. And that's why, whenever he appears, there are fans too young to remember him who lean across the fencing and shout '*Pou-pou ... Pou-pou!*'

16 SHAY ELLIOTT (1934–1971)

Many people have done it since — in fact for a while it was the established way. But Shay Elliott was first to come from this side of the Channel to join the ACBB, the Boulogne-Billancourt club in Paris.

Over the years it became a nursery for English-speaking riders, and its links with Peugeot often worked as a shoehorn to slip into sponsorship there. Tom Simpson, Stephen Roche, Phil Anderson ('Skippy' to the French, after a television kangaroo) and Robert Millar are those who've done it since.

Those nursery clubs are few now. But then, Micky Weigant was looking for new talent and saw the round-faced Irishman, who always looked out of place in less innocent surroundings, in the Route de France. In those days that was the amateur Tour de France and Elliott was doing well. Weigant took Elliott into the club.

Elliott got on well in France and made friends quickly. Before long he met a man who looked as sinister as Elliott looked innocent — Jean Stablinski. The Frenchman had been born Jean Stablewski, of Polish origins, but the French papers could never spell his name during the Peace Race and in the end he gave up an unequal battle.

Stablinski was French professional champion in 1960, 1962, 1963 and 1964, won Paris–Brussels in 1963, and became world champion at Salo in 1962. He was an influential ally, and, what's more, he also had a sister. She and Elliott quickly fell in love and they married. The union was happy to begin with, but it did bring an eccentric, not to say difficult, mother-in-law.

Stablinski's mother wanted to mollycoddle him. She didn't think cycle racing was a safe occupation for her only son, especially when her husband had died and left her alone but for Jean, and she tried to keep him at home. Stablinski, reading the situation well, figured that what she needed was a second husband. So he advertised for one.

He was lucky, and Mama Stablinski remarried and had a daughter. And Stablinski was lucky, too, because the man had a daughter of his own, and she and Stablinski fell in love and also got married. This complicated relationship wove Elliott still more closely to the Frenchman, and he spent much of his career riding either openly, or, more usually, illicitly, in his service.

Stablinski was a rough man with a permanent five o'clock shadow. He might have worked down the mines if the bike hadn't saved him. He won two stages of the Peace Race, when the Peace Race was a race ridden by rough-house eastern Europeans, Mongolians and anybody else who thought he could survive hours of cobbles, broken roads, elbows and shoving shoulders. He had an ability for stage races — he won the Tour of Belgium — but his talent was stronger in single-day races.

While Elliott became a servant to him, Stablinski allied himself to Jacques Anquetil. But while neither Anquetil nor Elliott were likely world-championship winners, Stablinski was. And in 1962, with Elliott's help, he became one.

There are many who said it should more rightly have been the Irishman's title. Even the French journalist Pierre Chany, not a man to overlook the merits of a Frenchman, concedes that Elliott that day 'was in super condition.' Elliott had won his country's first *maillot jaune*, in the 1963 Tour de France, and the *Het Volk* late-winter classic in Belgium. In 1962 he was third in the Tour of Spain. Such a man, in a break in the world championship and with a sprint like an Curragh racehorse, was not to be overlooked.

The 1962 race was on the banks of the river Garde at Salo. Stablinski was no expert tactician and he often wasted his energy attacking brutally without benefit. But this time he was lucky. With Elliott alongside to watch his interests, he got into a break with the German cyclo-cross expert Rolf Wolfshohl and the Belgian Jos Hoevenaers.

Stablinski feinted an attack which got Wolfshohl and Hoevenaers scrambling after him. Then he sent Elliott up the road instead. Again the other two had to respond, tiring themselves. Elliott — by far the best sprinter of the four — nevertheless obliged at the finish and allowed Stablinski to escape. The Frenchman became world champion, Elliott was second at 1-22 and Hoevenaers came in a further 22 seconds afterwards. France should have been more grateful to the Irishman's sacrifice. Stablinski was retired and standing in the crowd at Sallanches in 1980 before a Frenchman (Hinault) again won the pro road title.

You never knew whether Elliott was happy or simply wry. He had an enigmatic smile which tripped across his face like a little smirk.

But there were certainly odd stories. In London–Holyhead, at that time the longest unpaced race in the world, he felt the urgent call of nature. But it was more than a pee that he needed, and — in his own words — he 'popped into the bushes for a bloody big crap.'

This was rather more subtle than a Spaniard in the same event who hitched down his shorts and performed the same task on the move. 'It was awful,' recalled Roger St Pierre. 'It went all over his bike, all over his spokes, and because they were going downhill at the time and the wheels were turning quite fast, the stuff sprayed up everywhere.'

The talking point that London–Holyhead produced was the photographs of the finish. Tom Simpson crossed the line first but Elliott clearly had his fingers over his brake levers before he had reached the line. Suggestions that he had sold the race abounded. Vin Denson said afterwards that there had been an agreement among many of the Continental visitors that Simpson would win, in return for a pay-off; the plot had started to go wrong when Albert Hitchen came charging through the group at the finish — Elliott was braking to hold the Yorkshireman out of Simpson's way.

Elliott frequently admitted in private that he made more money by arranging other people's victories than by staging his own. He patently rode for Jean Stablinski in the world championship, surrendering his own chances. And later Stablinski tried to return the favour. But Elliott never had the success he gave to others.

His relationship with Stablinski's sister also floundered. And as his marriage waned, so did his successes. He could have achieved more, much more. But while there's more than one way of making a living on a bike, to ride for others depends on their continued patronage. When they fade, or fall from favour, you're left only with a likeable reputation as a workhorse, or perhaps mercenary, but none of the powers that made you so remarkable in the first place.

Who knows whether Elliott might have earned more if he'd ridden right from the start in his own interests? Who even knows, when English was rare in cycling and Irish-tinted English even more so, whether it could have been possible? He was an oddity who made an odd living. And when the living grew worse, he fell into hard times and made a few hundred pounds by selling stories of cycling scandals, sold races and drugs to a Sunday newspaper in Britain.

It was his last foolish move. It finally ruined his marriage.

'I knew times were hard for him at home,' Jock Wadley said at the time, 'but nobody knew just how hard until they realised he had had to do that.' Professional cycling has never taken kindly to having its secrets revealed. And as the Continental press had always been more circumspect or perhaps even less inquiring — reporters often feeling their own interests were tied up in 'protecting' their sport — the British revelations came as a blow.

Elliott was never forgiven. His career ended promptly. Those close to him say that the failed marriage, coupled with financial worries, were too much. He was found dead alongside a shotgun at his home in Dublin.

Roger St Pierre said: 'Shay was the last man you'd expect to commit suicide. He was a very even guy. There were no highs or lows. He wasn't tempestuous. He was just what one expects of the Irish — an easy-going, thoroughly likeable guy.'

17 LOUISON BOBET (1925–1983)

Poulidor … Anquetil … Géminiani … They were names from a golden era of French cycling. The French have never been as enthusiastic about their sport since, even with the likes of Bernard Hinault to dominate for them. Because Hinault was a different sort of winner, a businessman, talented but remote and efficient.

The other *vedette* of the era is one of a pair of brothers. Jean Bobet was gentle and philosophical. He learned English in Britain and loved to speak it. Brother Louison was a harder type — and more successful. And to find his soul, you have visit a village of maybe 4,000 souls. I passed through there once on that old Carlton, the back wheel laden with camping gear and the detritus of a fortnight's holiday.

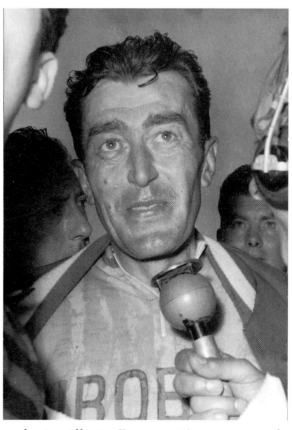

St-Méen-le-Grand is no more than a large village. Even so it's a crossroads and the administrative head of the canton of Ille-et-Vilaine, which gives it a local importance. The kind of place you pay your taxes, go to get married. Anything more important and you'd have to go into nearby Rennes.

Walk the rue de Montfort and you'll find the G. Dube clothing shop on a corner, next to a *patissier*. In 1925 it too was a bread shop, and Louison Bobet was born on one of the upper two floors on March 12.

Raphaël Géminiani called him 'the most courageous rider I've known.'

This is Brittany, where people feel as French as the Welsh feel English. They are normally proud of their own. Walk a little further to the Hôtel Central and ask for Mme Prigent; she will show you her collection of Bobet photographs. Still further and there's the Louison Bobet sports centre. The postmaster, Raymond

Quérat, asked to work in St-Méen because Bobet was his hero. Among those who were around at the time, he's not forgotten.

But those there now? Well, according to Michel Nail-Challal of *L'Equipe*, they certainly *have* forgotten. There used to be a Prix Souvenir-Louison-Bobet. It started in St-Méen-le-Grand the first year, and, ever since, the town's leaders have refused a repeat performance. They say it is too expensive.

And away from St-Méen-le-Grand there are also few who talk of Louison Bobet warmly.

Bobet was the first man to win the Tour de France three times in a row — in 1953, 1954 and 1955. The last time, he finished with a saddle boil, and, so the legend goes, came close to dying on the operating table. He was noted for his iron will and an equally inflexible grasp of his money. He died a prosperous man, of cancer.

Brian Robinson, who rode in the same era, said: 'Bobet was not easy to approach. He was a private man really and a little bit moody. He would soon sulk if things were not going right for him.

'Once, after the Tour finished, I had no contracts for seven days so I had a week off and went to a training camp at Epernay, where Bobet liked to rest and build up again. There weren't many miles involved, and I was told that if I sprinted for every kilometre sign for seven days, I would have the speed for the criteriums. I was steaming in the criterium and had taken every prime when Bobet came up to me. "If you don't let me win, you won't get another contract."

'He had so much control. He was Mr Cycling. I was getting £40 a criterium and he was getting £1,000. He was there at every race.'

Sporting Cyclist's René de la Tour said of him: 'He didn't look too good on the bike' and accused him of having the legs of a footballer rather than a pedaller — although it seems to have done Bobet no harm. The first time he rode the Tour de France, he vanished from the bunch across the Vars and Izoard to win by more than five minutes at Briançon. It is hard to dismiss such a man.

In 1954, at Solingen in West Germany, the seemingly stingy Louison Bobet became the first French world professional road champion for nearly 20 years — Antonin Magne having been the last in 1936. It was a victory he needed to overcome accusations that he had almost reached the sport's pinnacles but not quite.

It was Charles Pélissier's idea that he should dedicate his season. By then the old *routier* was working for *Miroir Sprint*, following the Tour de France as a journalist. After the stage into Nice, his interview with Bobet turned into advice.

'In your condition, there's nobody around who could beat you,' he told Bobet. 'Forget about the criteriums after the Tour, or most of them, and start training to become champion of the world.'

According to Pélissier, Bobet didn't commit himself immediately. That wasn't the way Bobet did things. Instead, he nodded silently, and a few minutes later the interview was over.

Solingen has been a steel town since the Middle Ages, first making swords and then knives and machinery. Its circuit is called the Klingen-Ring, a hard course at any time but made worse on Sunday, September 1, 1954, by what the French call *temps de chien* — or to translate it equally colourfully, weather unfit for a dog.

The wind howled and the rain sloshed down the side of the Belhaussen climb, the main difficulty. On the line, Bobet confessed to his manager, Daniel Dousset, that he knew it was his last chance to match Fausto Coppi, the Italian who was also out to win and had even declined the Tour de France with the public explanation that he was saving himself for the championship.

After five hours there were few left. Bobet attacked ten times in two laps, throwing himself at the circuit's two hills. Coppi was with him, and so were the little Luxembourgeois climber Charly Gaul and the man that Bobet most came to hate, Jacques Anquetil. And Anquetil was there to profit, not to protect.

Bobet attacked for the tenth time, and Coppi, exhausted, crashed into Gaul and felled both of them. The Frenchman, who saw nothing of the accident, cleared the summit of Belhaussen with just the Swiss Schaer for company. Well, company, yes, but Schaer was reduced to hanging on, exhausted but gleeful at this unexpected turn of events.

Yet soon he would be happier still.

Bobet and the Swiss were followed by their two team cars. In the French car, mechanic Paul Delaye was peering through the rain and wheel-spray, his cupped hand drawn across his brow to protect his eyes. What he saw could never have been predicted. As Bobet rode, his back wheel was shedding spokes by the moment.

Delaye leapt from the car before it had stopped. Schaer found sudden new energy and drove himself without forgiveness towards the line and fame, just 15km ahead. And Bobet, his cotton cap reversed, his hands in water-grey chamois mitts, waited disbelieving while Delaye pushed the new large-flanged rear wheel into its sockets.

And then Bobet set off again. His head drooped, his shoulders arched, and stroke by stroke he pounded down on the cranks. Inch by inch he wore down Schaer until two kilometres from the line he caught him. And immediately he attacked again.

It was all over for Schaer. The physical exertion, and then the mental drain of having glory snatched in the last mile and a half, were too much. Bobet, his face ghostly and drawn, crushed him and left him.

It took a long time for Bobet to recover. Helpers, fans and anyone else who could get to him massed about him, shouting, tugging, pushing, someone wiping his face, someone else draping a tracksuit jacket across the blue French jersey.

Bobet stood for a while, walked without his bike to wipe his face again, and then made his way to stand on the rostrum for the *Marseillaise*. Only then, according to those who were there, did colour return to his face. And only once he had returned to the team hotel did he speak to reporters.

He said: 'You can't imagine how much I suffered to get back to Schaer after my wheel went. I thought I had lost it. I thought I had lost a title that I deserved. Not for anything in the world would I relive that chase.

'God, that was hard. You need to have suffered on a bike to understand.' He left that night with a rainbow jersey in his suitcase.

Bobet wasted little of the money that success brought. It was normal then for cyclists to spend as they went as if their careers would last for ever. The pub and garage trades of out-of-the-way places were stiff with men whose faded glories were celebrated only by toothy framed photographs. But not Bobet. He put his earnings into the Institute of Thalassotherapy sea-cure centre at Quiberon, an island village off the Brittany coast between Lorient and Vannes. There was enough left over to fly a private plane, a toy which only millionaires enjoyed.

The footnote to this story is that the postmaster who asked to work in Bobet's birthplace finally despaired of the way his hero was ignored. In 1991 the Tour de France passed through St-Méen-le-Grand and observed the usual formalities. There was a short rush of nostalgia about the old Breton and then nothing more. Inspired, Raymond Quérat wrote a letter to *Ouest-France*, suggesting Bobet's fans write to him.

Hundreds of letters, films and photographs arrived. And on March 13, 1993, the exhibition which they made possible opened. More than a thousand people, two radio stations and a television network were there.

'St-Méen has rediscovered just how great a champion was born within its walls,' Quérat said.

18 CHARLY GAUL (1932–)

That little man who chased Bobet through the rain in Germany is still around. You don't hear much from him, but he keeps in touch with the sport which gave him a brief but brilliant living. He owed his name to the hills.

Until the bicycle, there were no roads at all across the Pyrénées and Alps. Who would want to cross them? And why? Even with the invention of the car, it was years before an engine could survive the gradient, the hours of toil and rarefied atmosphere. The only crossings were paths, beaten out by farmers with their sheep.

The routes were mapped, but they were of little interest to the Tour. The race could go only where the railways went. If it crossed the mountains it left the officials at the last station before the ascent. The riders began their work and the organisers boarded a train for the finish.

It's worth reflecting how much part the Tour de France played in motoring history. In 1910, Henri Desgrange brought the Pyrénées into the route for the first time. Never one to stint on other's labours — early stages started before midnight and ended at tea-time the following afternoon — he placed the Aubisque on a 330km haul from Luchon. And, delighted that a posh if straining car was available to take him to the summit, he set off with his partners. And there he waited.

It is Tour legend what happened next. The Aubisque was 5,610 feet high, crossed only by rocky trails. Dismayed, Desgrange and company waited and waited. They waited so long that they concluded their competitors had gone astray or fallen down a ravine. Desgrange was about to give up when a lone rider struggled painfully towards him. He couldn't speak and he passed in resentful silence.

A quarter of an hour later, Octave Lapize came the same way.

'What's happened? Where are the others?' Desgrange demanded.

Lapize said nothing. He leaned on his bike with one arm on the saddle, the other on the bars. For a while he stared silently at Desgrange and his city swells through reddened eyes. And then, with effort, he hissed just one word: 'Murderers!'

Times change, of course, and the roads improve with them. But the first mountain-top finishes weren't until 1952, at Mont Genèvre, the Alpe d'Huez, and the Puy de Dôme — just in time for a little man from Pfaffenthal in Luxembourg. His name was Charly Gaul.

In those days, little winged climbers could do astonishing things. Now it's remarkable if the stars get away at all. That they should soar clear alone and pedal to the top in glory is unthinkable. I'm not sure why.

Charly Gaul was 57 minutes behind on general classification going into the Alps in 1955. By Paris he was up to third place. In 1956 his climbing was so brilliant that he moved up 41 places in a week and a half.

If Bahamontes was the Eagle of Toledo, Gaul was the Angel of the Mountains. Bahamontes bore a permanent worried, perplexed air, as if the world were a toil and a puzzle. Which sometimes it was. But Gaul, in repose at least, had a cherubic appearance, like Paul McCartney — or Lucien van Impe and Stephen Roche. That's what gave him his nickname.

Now, think of the bottom gear you'd choose if you were really scared of the mountains. Now lower it a bit. That's what Gaul rode. Great soupdishes of sprockets nestled against his back wheel. He could rev like a schoolboy time-triallist.

But if he looked like a schoolboy, he could behave like one as well. He was a little flea who got on everyone's nerves. Those who rode with him complained that he made up in ego what he lacked in inches. He lolled about lazily on the flat stages — although he could be a formidable time-triallist and more than once beat Anquetil — and went to pieces with heatstroke if the sun came up. But give him a cool, or better still a wet, dreadful day in the mountains, and he gloried.

Roger St Pierre, for whom he was an early hero, said: 'Tactically naive, Charly Gaul often gave away many minutes on the flat stages, but once into the mountains he became a true master of his craft. At his best in bad conditions, when pouring rain added extra misery to the tortuous uphill gradients, he climbed with a fluid, easy, fast-pedalling style, dancing lightly on the pedals or sitting comfortably, hands relaxed holding just above the brake-lever tops.'

But don't take a photograph of Gaul from those days to search for him on the streets of Luxembourg. He still lives there, but something has happened to the Angel since. His feet are more firmly on the ground. He's become a chubby man with a beard, unrecognisable when he visited the Tour de France last time it entered the tiny duchy.

So different does he look that a French magazine ran a picture of him fishing by a lake and invited its readers to guess who this out-of-shape character could be. Nobody wonders at Rik van Steenbergen putting on a few pounds — but surely not that tiny man who darted up hillsides to everybody else's dismay?

Gaul won the Tour mountain title twice, in 1955 and 1956, and in 1958 he won the Tour itself, leaving Bahamontes to take the mountains. A year later Gaul defended the mountains and added the race.

He was 23 in 1955, old enough for strength but young enough to be light. Folk knew who he was, of course: the previous autumn he'd come third to Louison Bobet in the world championship in Germany and become Luxembourg's *Sportler des Jahres*, sportsman of the year, for the first of five times. It was another of those wonderfully wet days that he loved.

But knowing someone's a good climber and being able to do something about it are two different things. Coupled to that, Gaul was well enough down in the 1955 Tour that he could be given a solo with no risk of disrupting the tune.

The first day in the Alps reached from Thonon-les-Bains to Briançon. It opened with the col de Télégraphe. I shouldn't think anybody worried much that the Dutchman Jan Nolten made an early attempt. And Gaul showed little emotion as he switched into his 27-tooth sprocket and passed him. Others watched with unexcited interest. But by the top, Gaul had five minutes — enough to be taken seriously but still no threat. The risk came on the Galibier that followed. Untired by the Télégraphe, he rode still harder up the Galibier and had all but three seconds of a quarter of an hour's lead at the top.

By now there were great alarm bells ringing. Gaul had wiped out all but a few minutes of his deficit on Bobet.

The beak-nosed Ferdy Kübler — still an alert and dapper old-timer in Zürich who handles public relations for the Tour of Switzerland — arched his back and bent his Coppi-like legs in chase. But he could whittle back only a minute, and Gaul kept his third place to the capital.

But it did have to be a cold day. He once struggled at four miles an hour through a snowstorm in the Giro d'Italia to win a stage. But in that same Tour de France of 1955, Bobet dropped him across the cruelly hot Mont Ventoux and guaranteed himself victory. A whole handful of unexciting climbers reached the Ventoux's summit before Gaul. And in 1957 the Tour proved so warm that he didn't even get to see the mountains, still less ride over them.

And then came 1958, the year that he won. He averaged 22.8mph, the fastest the race had been ridden. His lead was 3-10, much the same as his deficit three years earlier.

First he beat Anquetil in the time-trial at Chateaulin in Brittany. And then in the Chartreuse — again one of the scenes of Eddy Merckx's history — came Gaul's stage for a Wagnerian opera.

Chartreuse is shorthand for the hills that surround it. It's simpler than listing climbs which in themselves are far less significant than the Galibier but which, one after the other like sawteeth, cripple both legs and lungs. Worse, the Lautaret, Luitel, Porte, Cucheron and Granier followed two days of harder climbs.

The hills are high and the clouds were low. Gaul walked to his hotel window that morning and stared at the darkness. He smiled. He'd rested, eaten and been massaged along with the other members of the Luxembourg mixed-nations team. He rode to the start in his red, white and blue jersey with his team car behind him. Things were looking well.

The stage ran from Briançon to Aix-les-Bains. He went straight to the front. Moving up and down that big block, he twitched and taunted the bunch on the Luitel. But as yet there was no panic, because the overnight tactical talks had concluded that Raphaël Géminiani was the big threat after taking the yellow jersey the night before. Géminiani was one of those who had the talent and the brains to win the Tour but had won neither that nor a world championship. That he would let go of the jersey without an epic tussle was unthinkable.

Gaul was too far back to be a worry. The decision, therefore, was that he was a risk only to those who also wanted to be king of the mountains. Géminiani would go with him as far as he could, but that was no worry because Gem was a fair climber and Gaul had no cause to overdo things. Others likely to follow would be profiteers who thought a leg-up at Gaul's expense would lift them a few rungs.

And that's the way the thinking stayed. Until Gaul tore it apart. After the Luitel, he repeated the agony for those who still thought they could stay with him. Géminiani rode to a sea of weakness to preserve his yellow jersey. And then Gaul was alone.

Géminiani and Anquetil chased him through the lowlands between the Isère and Grenoble. Behind them, Bobet, Dotto and Adriaenssens were in another group. But Gaul was gone. Anquetil was taken ill on the col du Porte and Géminiani lost time with a damaged pedal, but that does nothing to lessen Gaul's victory. He won by eight minutes.

Anquetil had won the previous year's Tour by 15 minutes at his first try; in this one stage Gaul stung him for 23 minutes. Anquetil quit next day with a lung infection.

They called Gaul *Engel der Berge* in Luxembourg. In 1951 the duchy picked him for the amateur Tour of Austria, and Gaul confessed: 'Until then I'd never in my life seen anything higher than 800 metres. And I looked at the route sheet and saw that on the fourth stage we were riding across the Grossglockner, which is 2,505 metres.' Undeterred, Gaul finished ahead and alone — in rain and sleet.

But climbers have brief careers. Gaul was a pro from 1953 to 1965. He was king of the mountains in France in 1955 for the first and took the title for the last time in Italy in 1959. Like Bahamontes, he was brief but brilliant.

19 JOOP ZOETEMELK (1946–)

I had a choice now. I could go north or I could catch the train south. I'd fancied seeing Freddy Maertens, not least because anyone who's gone from 50-odd wins a year to disaster and then to world champion for a second time before disappearing into a marsh of obscurity must have a tale to tell. So I rang.

It took a while to explain who I was and what I wanted. We got as far as arranging a date when Maertens produced evidence that he's still struggling to pay off his tax demands.

'It'll cost 5,000 francs,' he said.

I didn't have 5,000 francs or anything like it. I was looking for the words when he said something extraordinary.

'Maximum,' he said.

Maertens, poor chap, was so stuck for cash that he was prepared to start bidding against himself before I'd even spoken. I felt sorry for him, but I still didn't have 5,000 francs, maximum or not.

I did have a pile of five-franc pieces, though, and I spent half of them getting Joop Zoetemelk's number in Paris and then the other half establishing that he wasn't there. That disappointed me just as much.

I chatted to Joop Zoetemelk once in Holland, before the Tour de France, and again before a race from Bristol to Bradford. The Tour that year started in Leiden, the university town close to The Hague, where he was born on December 3, 1946.

I mentioned that I'd been charmed to see him riding one weekend not in something hugely important but in the Dutch club team time-trial championship. I forget even whether the Swift club won — it was simply that one of the best riders in the world should give up a weekend to repay old friendships.

He looked almost lost for words — as he so often is — as though it had never occurred to him that he *shouldn't* take part.

'Of course,' he said. 'I have many friends in my club.'

There are canals that run through Leiden and The Hague, and in a good winter they freeze. Winter skating is a big sport in Holland, and Zoetemelk was good enough to be a regional champion in his teens. Those who remember him say he was no more boastful or talkative than now.

That someone so patently friendly and approachable should have had such a bad press over the years seems unfair. Like Poulidor — for whom he first rode as a professional — he made the second rung of the Tour de France a possession. And even when he won, in 1980, it wasn't with universal glory ringing in his ears.

The Tour in 1980 was the Battle of Bernard's Knee. It had been the theme of the race from its first days, and gallons of ink were dedicated to the tendinitis that caused the problem. Would the dark-haired, grey-flecked Breton Bernard Hinault suffer because of it? Would he win despite it? A nation given to ideas rather than conclusions could make much of a puzzle like that.

Hinault had the *maillot jaune* at Pau, within sight of the Pyrénées, when he began politely declining interviews in his hotel bedroom. When the journalists returned, they found him gone, vanished into the night. Nobody would say to where, although it clearly wasn't anywhere to do with the Tour de France. They phoned his home. They called on regional colleagues to drive into Yffiniac. But there was no sign.

They traced him before long to a team-mate's home at Lourdes, the neighbouring town. There was a pleasing completion of the circle amid the unspoken Catholicism of cycle racing that Hinault should be so close to both the Pyrénées and the shrine at which miracles happened when he fell foul of his knee.

He was unrepentant. He was fed up with his knee, he was fed up with the attention it was getting. He was fed up, above all, at the prospect of not winning the Tour de France again. Could he kindly be left alone to get on with his misery in private?

That left Zoetemelk in the ascendancy. The vice-president had been dragged out to run the country. His thinning red hair makes him look older than he is. But the truth is that he was 33 and relying on his Raleigh team-mates. Cynics say he preferred to rely on others to make errors in his favour rather than commit himself. Unlike so many Dutchmen, he speaks fluent French but poor English, which made him relaxed in France. But not so relaxed that he could cope with suggestions that he would win the Tour merely through default.

'Surely,' he reasoned with increasing frustration, 'winning the Tour de France or any other sporting event is a question of health and robustness? If

Hinault doesn't have that health and robustness and I have, that makes me a valid winner.'

The world — or rather the French, because in the Tour de France that's much the same thing — declined to come to a conclusion. And before long Hinault had come back and won another three times, and everybody forgot about the Dutchman and left him to live in retirement with his French wife in Paris.

He'd come so close to it before. In 1971 it was Merckx and not Hinault who had him by the ear. The Frenchman Christian Raymond dubbed Merckx 'le cannibal' — a man who more wanted to eat men than simply beat them — and it stuck. It stuck because it was appropriate.

It was Zoetemelk's rough luck that he always had to fight such men. But Merckx, like Hinault, wasn't faultless. In the Chartreuse valley in the 1971 Tour, Merckx had an off-day. The little Spaniard Luis Ocana — as much French as Spanish, which made him a general hero — decided to make mischief. He cleared off with Bernard Thévenet, the promising but ultimately disappointing Swede Gosta Petterson (strongest of the brothers who'd formed the Swedish team time-trial squad), and Zoetemelk.

Ocana was delighted, Merckx demoralised ... and Zoetemelk in yellow.

That in itself was news. What made it better was that Ocana did it again next day in the Alps. And again Zoetemelk went with him. Merckx crept over the line at Orcière Merlette with his face etched by exhaustion. Ocana had dropped him by five minutes and Merckx was not amused.

Next day he took revenge. Journalists got wind of a story that night and found his mechanics preparing his bikes in their garage. By the morning both Ocana and Zoetemelk had cause to worry. Merckx attacked Ocana relentlessly, and rode the Spaniard off his wheel and made him chase him for 250km. Ocana was humiliated, exhausted. Two days later Merckx did it again under a sky leaden black with curtains of rain. He took Ocana on a devil's ride through the Pyrénées, and eventually Ocana fell off his bike on the col de Mente. Zoetemelk crashed into him and Ocana ended the day barely conscious in hospital. Within a year and a half he had left the sport.

Merckx took back his lead (although he declined for a day to wear the yellow jersey, as a tribute to Ocana's bravery) and no more was heard of Zoetemelk.

The point of this story is that his critics say Zoetemelk was an opportunist, a man who gazed at the crown but never summoned the nerve to grab it. His pale skin and propensity to sunburn led to a joke even among the Dutch. Why, they asked, did he never get a suntan? Answer: because he was always in someone else's shadow.

It is a claim that angers his countryman Rini Wagtmans, whom I met the day after seeing Wim van Est.

At his clothing factory in St Willebrord he told me: 'Joop Zoetemelk is the best rider that the Netherlands has ever known. There has never been a better one. From the end of the sixties until the start of the eighties, he was at the top of European racing. But he was never a team leader.

'Joop could not give instructions. He was treated and helped with respect. But when Zoetemelk won the Tour for Raleigh in 1980, the instructions had to come from Knetemann and Raas. And van der Velde, come to that.

'Zoetemelk was a really nice man who was actually too nice for the bike. He couldn't command.'

I asked him about Zoetemelk's reputation as a wheel-sucker.

'No,' he said. 'All that talk of being a *wielzuiger* is lies. Total lies. Joop is the best rider of all time in Holland. And he could ride tremendously well alone. He could win a time-trial. But Joop was economical on the bike. And that is why he could ride until he was 40 [Zoetemelk was 38 when he won the world championship in 1985].

'He is the only rider who has ridden against three generations — Merckx, Hinault and LeMond. And he has ridden against Thévenet and Ocana. And how many people have overlapped so many generations? Zoetemelk is one of the few, along with Poulidor, *ja?*'

Zoetemelk agrees. He told reporters once: 'They all tried to duel with Eddy. He killed them. I was smarter. I refused to force myself. I knew exactly how far my talents reached. The others thought they could go further than that. It was enough for me to stay with him. You can't imagine the strength he had in his legs.'

In fact Zoetemelk had the equal of Merckx more often than his critics recall. He was often the better climber, as he proved in the 1974 Paris–Nice, which he won. In fact he might well have gone on to win the Tour de France in the same year, except that he crashed into a British car left unattended at the finish of a stage of the Midi-Libre stage race. His temple cracked under the impact. Zoetemelk was taken to hospital in Béziers. It looked uncertain that he would ever think straight again, let alone ride a bike. Yet nine months later he again won Paris–Nice — only to catch meningitis, lose a reputed 10kg in a week and come close to dying. He never fully got over it, and the head injury still affects his sense of taste.

But the point I made to Wagtmans was that it wasn't simply the Dutch who called Zoetemelk a leech but Eddy Merckx himself — and Merckx had been Wagtman's boss in the Molteni team.

'*Ja*, that used to be said in the sixties. In 1970 Joop Zoetemelk rode his first Tour de France. And if you are like a young animal that's been let loose, then of course you're afraid. You're scared of the unknown.

'If you then ride the Tour de France and you're second, after the *superkampioen* Merckx, then Merckx can't say Zoetemelk was a wheel-sucker because the lad had just ridden naturally. His lack of knowledge just made him uncertain.

'When you ride over the Tourmalet, or the col d'Aubisque, or the Télégraphe, for the first time, then you don't know what's going to happen to you. You get knocked with a hammer, then again, and then again. And by the time you get over the top, you've died seven deaths. You've had your head down on the handlebar tape seven times. And you're scared to take the initiative. But Joop is a great rider, and a great sportsman, and a great man as well.'

What Holland needed was a hero. It had done nothing before the war. There were a few afterwards — Valentijn, van Schendel and Middelkamp — but apart from Middelkamp's world championship in 1947, they were still outclassed internationally. Even Wim van Est was a false dawn.

Jan Janssen marked the new start with the 1968 Tour de France. Zoetemelk won Paris–Nice in 1974 and 1975, Jan Raas won Milan–San Remo in 1977, Gerrie Knetemann became world champion on the Nürburgring in 1978 and won Paris–Nice next spring, and then in 1979 Gerrie Knetemann took the world championship.

But the world judges a nation and its riders only by the Tour de France. And it took Zoetemelk a long time.

Maybe I've dwelled too long on Zoetemelk's critics. Nobody carps at Raymond Poulidor for running permanently second to Jacques Anquetil, after all. And Zoetemelk both held the yellow jersey and won the Tour de France, which is more than Poulidor ever did. So let me make amends.

If you list all the Tour de France results from the first 90 years, you can calculate the best of all time by giving them points for how they finished — 10 to the winner, nine for the runner-up and so on. As you can see from the table on page 138, Zoetemelk heads that list. Merckx is only sixth.

In 1983, drugs testers caught Zoetemelk taking steroids for the second time. It demoralised him so much that he retired. He stayed out a year, decided he liked racing too much, and rode for the last time in 1985. His remarkable success was the world championship at Montello. He was old enough to need permission from the Union Cycliste Internationale to ride as a veteran.

Bizarrely for a man quite incapable of acceleration, he leapt away on the last corner. There was a mile to go. The others watched LeMond, and Zoetemelk said he was trying to force the American's hand and provide a lead-out for the other

Dutchmen, van der Velde and van der Poel. Unfortunately for them and the local Italian, Moreno Argentin, LeMond did nothing at all. Zoetemelk had a hundred yards and saw no reason not to keep it. To make matters worse for the others, LeMond reacted at the last moment and came second.

Zoetemelk lives now with his wife Françoise, with whom he established a 40-room hotel called Le Richemont at Meaux, on the Marne. Appropriately, Françoise's father was an executive of the Tour de France. Zoetemelk would consider he has won the race's greatest prize.

Tour de France results from first 90 years (see page 137)

Position	Rider	Country	Points
1	Joop Zoetemelk	Holland	94
2	Raymond Poulidor	France	76
3	Lucien van Impe	Belgium	70
4	Bernard Hinault	France	68
5	Gustave Garrigou	France	66
6	Eddy Merckx	Belgium	64
=7	Jacques Anquetil	France	58
=7	Antonin Magne	France	58
=9	Nicolas Frantz	Luxembourg	51
=9	Greg LeMond	USA	51
11	Louison Bobet	France	49
12	Gino Bartali	Italy	43
13	Joaquim Agostinho	Portugal	42
=14	François Faber	Luxembourg	40
=14	Firmon Lambot	France	40
=14	Jean Alavoine	France	40
17	Stan Ockers	Belgium	39
18	Bernard Thévenet	France	38
=19	André Leducq	France	37
=19	Laurent Fignon	France	37
=19	Federico Bahamontes	Spain	37

20 JAN DERKSEN (1919–)

So it had to be north. Peter Post had rung Jan Derksen for me when I was in Amstelveen all that time ago. The great old sprinter hadn't been able to see me. 'But do try again', he'd said. So I tried. And he was back.

'I'd be delighted to talk to an Englishman,' he said on the phone. We arranged a time, he gave me directions, and then I tried one of his contemporaries. Arie van Vliet was another part of the triumvirate that was completed with Reg Harris. van Vliet, too, would be delighted to talk to an Englishman, but not that particular week. He too was going away.

That cold that I'd caught in the lower bunk of the North Sea ferry was gone now and the wind had dropped. But the temperature had fallen too. A light frost clung to the hedges, and the light was clear across the polders, reminding me that nowhere in Holland does it ever seem you are quite out of one village before approaching the next. I needed gloves as I spent two days riding back north.

The Dutch divide Holland by the two rivers that cross it from east to west. Below the rivers, you're a bumpkin, little better than a Belgian. You'll be short, with dark hair, probably a Roman Catholic and a great enthusiast for beer, carnivals and having a good time.

Those below the river look north to the midlanders and call them arrogant and cold. Rotterdam, Amsterdam, The Hague and the other cities towards the coast have grown almost into one urban sprawl that gives the residents, so the southerners say, the ill manners and harsh accents of city-dwellers everywhere.

The midlanders, of course, look down on their superstitious, easy-going southern neighbours. But they're equally dismissive of those above the rivers, who are tall and blond and broad-shouldered and generally dim. By the time you get to the extreme north, they deny being Dutch at all and speak the ancient language of Friesland, which is as understandable to the rest of Holland as Gaelic is to English-speakers.

Jan Derksen lives in the midlands. He lives on the edge of Amsterdam, an extraordinary city with 100 kilometres of canals set in concentric semi-circles with the occasional linking waterway, so that from above they resemble a watery spider-web. He struck me as neither arrogant nor guttural. He is a pleasant old gent who lives on the bend of a side street under the flight path to Schiphol airport.

He's tall, upright, well-dressed, with thin grey hair. He greeted me in cardigan, white shirt with tie, and smart shoes. His house is large by Dutch standards. The white outside wall has a single word in cast-iron script as a title. It says 'Ordrup'. It's the track in Copenhagen. And linguistically talented though Dutchman are, he is nevertheless the only one I know who speaks Danish (as well as Italian, German, French and English).

Even in his 70s, he has the energy to watch the six-days of Europe. He's still in touch, fixing deals, arranging contacts.

But it puzzled me not simply that a man so current should pick a house name from the past, but that he shouldn't have chosen one of the tracks on which he became world sprint champion. Oerlikon would have been a good name. He won there in Zürich. Or Rocourt in Belgium. Or Milan, where he won as an amateur.

'Ah,' he said. 'But I won the big omnium in Copenhagen ten times, and that was more or less a world championship. That was where I raced most and where I was fondest of racing.' He rode there for the first time in 1938 and for the last in 1963. A year later, he stopped racing at 45.

You always get coffee in a Dutch house. Good coffee too. His wife brought it on a tray, and reminded her husband that he was due to visit their son, who was in hospital briefly. Unlike other champions, there was no sign of trophies from those days, no pictures. I wondered whether to mention it. It turned out the medals are in a bank vault; nothing's on display because thieves took the gold medal he won in the Grand Prix of Paris and broke his heart.

So I told him that Reg Harris had always spoken highly of him — to cheer him up — and that he'd had a picture of him on the windowsill of his study in Cheshire. And I told him, too, that I'd tried to see van Vliet, the other man in the picture. It was taken at a celebration meeting for the three pensionable properties, in Copenhagen and Zürich. Derksen would have liked one in London as well, but London had no track worthy of the name.

'Harris has stayed active for a long time, eh?' he said. It was only a short time before the old Manchester terrier died. 'Still training, I think. I rang him last year, but I didn't know until then that he was still riding. Oh yes, for four or five years he was really the best sprinter, but it was short. It was pure strength. van Vliet and me, we were more of the Screu type. No speed was too great.

'But for Harris, and for Hubner, it was like a motor with high compression. If you take your foot off the accelerator, it … *whoof!*' He lurched forward to mimic a rapid loss of speed.

'Harris had to keep stamping on the pedals. He rode so terribly hard. Harris was a colossal sprinter, but he lasted only a short time. In 1949 he was world champion for the first time, and I was second. In 1957, when I was world champion for the last time and Harris went out in the quarter-finals, we all thought what a short time Harris had been at the top.

'He is another type of rider. van Vliet and I could do other things. We rode madisons, we rode six-days and we rode on the road, but Harris was solely a sprinter. Absolutely nothing else.

'It's a question of your muscles, you see? We had suppleness, and he was totally a *krachtexplosie*, a strength explosion. Once the explosion had happened, he could manage absolutely nothing more. A schoolboy could go riding past him.'

Harris was furious when I reported these comments to him. I thought he might have been mildly amused. Derksen, after all, was making the point through exaggeration. But I could imagine Harris looking up the dialling code for Amsterdam to give the old boy a ticking-off.

Derksen poured more coffee, then answered a phone call in Italian. His voice rose as another KLM Boeing whistled overhead with its flaps and wheels down. He replaced the receiver.

'Against a rider like Harris, you always had to look out. For van Vliet and me, it was better if the sprint began earlier, so there was a longer lead. Harris wanted to slow it down, to stop, to stand still. So you had to use tactics against him.'

Every time he recalled races, he was there on the line. He didn't exactly duck and dive with his shoulders like an old boxer, but the nerves were taut, the brain looking for the feint, the bluff, the chance, the attack.

It was Arie van Vliet who challenged him most, of course. Harris kept himself in England when he wasn't under contract, whereas van Vliet was a short drive away. Harris was exotic, but Derksen and van Vliet were a sure draw for a domestic crowd.

'He was always my big rival,' he said with respect in his voice. 'We developed together. He was Olympic champion in 1936 in the kilometre, but after that we were always rivals, especially in the Dutch championship. Tremendous battles, they were, fighting, fighting. And the public knew that. They knew we were going to give everything we had to beat each other.'

In Derksen's day, the money was on the track. The road was something you tried if you couldn't make your living on the ovals or if you just didn't fancy it.

'The track was where you got your money — much more than on the road. On the road, there was only the Tour de France. When television came and all the advertising, and all the factory teams could see the way things were going, television and press attention went to the road sport. That is where the money and then the track riders went.

'So there were only just a few true track specialists left, plus a few road riders who also wanted to ride six-days. They weren't specialists, though, were they? There were a few exceptions who could do both, but most road riders couldn't manage more than, maximum, two or three sixes. More than that, they had to get permission from their teams, and their teams, of course, were paying them to get publicity on the road.'

Little of what Derksen earned came from sponsors. Harris had Raleigh, and when he retired he discovered he was being paid more than Raleigh's chairman, which made joining the company afterwards less comfortable than he'd hoped. But Derksen earned most from what spectators paid at the gate, passed on in appearance contracts.

'Don't get me wrong,' he said. 'It was still a lot of money that the riders earned, but not so much as now.'

To him, as to Harris, sprinting was an art. It had a style, it had nuances, it had technique. The road is little more than brute force by contrast.

'The people don't know what they're looking at now,' he said.

Derksen used to tune to Hilversum as a boy and listen to reporters talking from distant parts about the six-day races, just as I'd listened to Jock Wadley calling in to Network Three. He dreamed of being up there, and he'd ride a few miles and go to a training session. But not until he was 15, after his last school exams, did his father give him a proper racing bike.

Derksen recalled: 'I just stood there gazing at it.'

He took out a schoolboy licence from the KNWU, the national federation, and joined a club in Alkmaar. The town is at the start of a peninsula north of Rotterdam, and it's famous now for its quaint canals and the regular cheese market, where porters carry *bolletjes* of cheese balanced on boards on their head.

He went along that first day with a friend, and by his 18th birthday he was in the national team. A KNWU coach had spotted him on the town's little track.

'From there it all went fast. At 19 I was third in the world championship here in Amsterdam and a year later I was world amateur champion. That was in 1939.

In 1940 I was supposed to ride in the Olympics at Helsinki and I was picked for the sprint and the kilometre.

'It was as good as certain that I would win two gold medals, because I was already world champion, but then the war broke out.'

The Germans demanded to roll through Holland to invade Belgium from the north, rather than tackle the Belgians in the Ardennes. When Holland refused, the Luftwaffe demolished Rotterdam and promised to do the same elsewhere nightly until it changed its mind. The Dutch, who'd intended to stay neutral as they had in the first war, became an occupied nation.

Racing carried on for a while. The Germans might give permission to travel within the occupied territories and sometimes into Switzerland. But in 1942 the travelling stopped.

'There were a lot of small tracks here in Holland in those days, and you could always ride something — an omnium or something. Before 1942 you could get a visa and a stamp in your passport, and you could get a contract and you could ride in Denmark, for example. There wasn't much money, of course, and if you wanted to eat well then it was all buying on the black market, and that cost a heap of money. And you couldn't pay that. So we used to swap. A farmer would say you could have some butter if you would part with your watch, and I would get a watch from Switzerland and I'd do that, but you just couldn't get equipment.'

He never had a proper job. A brief spell in the bike trade, yes, 'learning about steel and so on,' but he was in the national team so early that he was a full-time athlete almost from the day he rode a bike.

Even when he stopped racing, he stayed in the business. He was the Dutch federation track coach for four years and went to the Tokyo and Mexico Olympics. He arranged riders for events at the Olympic stadium in Amsterdam, and once gave Graham Webb a ride with the national pursuit team. I've seen him at the Zürich six-day and again at Ghent.

All old-timers think things were better in their day, and Derksen's no exception. But he concedes that nothing can stay the same. Ron Webb changed six-days into simply racing-on-six-days when he transformed the event in London. Others scoffed but they soon copied. For one thing, it saved heating and staffing a stadium all but empty of spectators in the dull hours.

To me, things have gone further, and six-days seem sometimes little different from a Moulin Rouge on wheels — a sequence of entertaining events with little attempt at continuity. Derksen nodded as he listened, paused, and then replied.

'The people demand different things these days' he said. 'In the old days, they'd tolerate riders sitting down and resting their legs, and reading the papers, but not now. People were much more easily satisfied then. Now they want more racing and more speed, but it's still difficult to please the people.

'I was in Ghent and the racing there was tremendous and the crowd was really enthusiastic, but talk to them about the riders from the past and they say "*Ja*, they raced further and they raced longer — three to four hours," but that's not it. The truth is that these days, once the chase had been on for an hour or so, people would go off for a drink somewhere. People wouldn't sit for three or four hours these days, just watching.'

Derksen would. I'm sure he would. He'll still be watching bike racing until the day he dies. And he'll die happy because he's a bike rider. I know he will.

21 ZEG BEDANKT — EN TOT ZIENS!*

It took a while to do it. I felt old afterwards. I felt like I was living in the past, and that was wrong. The past wasn't better; it was simply different. And yet, because it was different, it becomes more interesting with age.

One day I shall go back and do it again. I'm too late to see Marcel Kint, who used to eat salted herrings on his training rides so that he'd get used to the thirst he'd experience in southern France. I'm too late to ask Jean Robic about the day he loaded his water bottles with lead shot so that he'd roll down the mountains faster. And if I'm not quick, I'll be too late to ask Briek Schotte what it was like to be a real Lion of Flanders, in the years when it rained every day and the mud swept across the cobbles in stripes of brown custard.

I did ring him, incidentally. I could go and see him, sure, but not quite then. And I rang Herman van Springel, whose son told me in perfect English 'I'm sorry, my father's not here at the moment but I can ask him to ring you back.' You can't see them all.

I still had the street map of Amsterdam and Amstelveen that the hotel had given me the day before I saw Peter Post. I used it to find the nearest office of the VVV, the national tourist organisation, and asked them to find me another hotel. And next day I rode back to Hoek van Holland.

I was thinking things over as I rolled up through Suffolk towards home. Were things different then? Or was I trying to grasp something that never quite existed? I was sitting in a Little Chef when I concluded that one day there'd be someone else like me seeking out the Chiapuccis and Indurains and drinking coffee with them and reminiscing with equal fascination.

But try as I might, I couldn't imagine they'd have the fun that I'd had.

I paid my bill, unlocked the white Carlton that was too small for me, and rode home.

---

* *Thanks … and see you again!*